DAVID LIVINGSTONE

The Unexplored Story

STEPHEN TOMKINS

LION

Published by Lion Books
an imprint of
Lion Hudson plc
Wilkinson House, Jordan Hill Road,
Oxford OX2 8DR, England
www.lionhudson.com/lion

ISBN 978 0 7459 5568 1
e-ISBN 978 0 7459 5719 7

First edition 2013

Acknowledgments

Every effort has been made to trace the original copyright holders where required. In some cases this has proved impossible. We shall be happy to correct any such omissions in future editions.

pp. 17, 24, 25, 80, 91, 95, 227: Extracts from *Mission and Empire* by Andrew Ross copyright © 2002 Andrew Ross. Reprinted by permission of Bloombury.

pp. 29, 34, 60, 63, 68, 69, 70, 71, 73, 74, 93, 97, 110: Extracts from *David Livingstone family letters 1841–1856* edited by Isaac Shapera copyright © Chatto & Windus, 1959. Reprinted by permission of Random House.

pp. 32, 36, 37, 40–41, 44, 45, 46, 48, 49, 50, 54, 55, 56, 57, 58, 60, 61, 65, 67, 68, 72, 74, 77, 79, 81, 88, 89, 90, 94, 96, 99, 100, 102, 109–10, 115, 116: Extracts from *Livingstone's Missionary Correspondence 1841–1856* edited by Isaac Shapera copyright © Chatto & Windus, 1961. Reprinted by permission of Random House.

pp. 34, 52, 72, 73, 81, 97, 105, 127, 177, 226, 229: Extracts from *David Livingstone* by Tim Jeal copyright © Tim Jeal, 1973. Reprinted by permission of Aitken Alexander Associates.

p. 134: Extract from *Kirk on the Zambesi: A chapter of African history* by Sir Reginald

Coupland © Sir Reginald Coupland, 1928. Reprinted by permission of Oxford University Press.

pp. 28, 30, 31, 32, 33, 44, 60, 63, 71, 94, 127: Extracts from London Missionary Society Archive, Africa Odds, '?', SOAS Library & Special Collections.

pp. 171, 172, 204, 208, 209, 210, 211, 212, 213, 214, 217: Extracts from *Livingstone's 1871 Field Diary* edited by Adrian S. Wisnicki sourced from Digital Library Program, University of California, Los Angeles.

pp. 34, 43, 44, 48, 54, 64, 65, 68, 69, 76, 77, 80, 81, 92, 122, 131, 135, 136, 137, 139, 142, 143, 145, 146, 155, 157, 168, 178, 179, 181, 187, 189: David Livingstone archive material from National Library of Scotland, Royal College of Physicians and Surgeons of Glasgow, Wellcome Library, Mitchell Library: James Cowie Collection, National Museum of the Royal Navy and Royal Geographical Society. Sourced from and used by permission of Livingstone Online.

pp. 19, 53, 56, 60, 63, 106, 110, 112, 120, 125, 126, 127, 130, 131, 132, 133, 136, 137, 139, 141, 145, 146, 147, 148, 149, 152, 161, 166, 167–68, 172, 174, 175, 178, 179, 183, 193, 203, 223, 227, 229: Sourced from *David Livingstone: His life and letters* by George Seaver. Published by HarperCollins, 1957.

pp. 31, 59, 130, 131, 132, 133, 134, 136, 138, 139–40, 141, 142, 144, 148, 152, 163, 164, 169, 170: Sourced from *The Zambesi Journals and Letters of Dr John Kirk 1858–63* edited by Reginald Foskett. Published by Oliver & Boyd, 1965.

pp. 168, 171, 179: Sourced from *The Zambesi Journal of James Stewart, 1862–1863* edited by J. Wallis. Published by Chatto & Windus, 1952.

pp. 132, 178: Sourced from *Livingstone, the liberator: A study of a dynamic personality* by James MacNair. Published by HarperCollins, 1968.

A catalogue record for this book is available from the British Library

Printed and bound in Great Britain, December 2012, LH26

CONTENTS

Chapter 1

THE MILL

From the old photograph, the mill in the industrial village of Blantyre, on the Clyde, eight miles south-east of Glasgow, looks like a prison. Five storeys of pale blank wall, with square towers, it dominates the village as it dominated the lives of the villagers. Before Shaftesbury's Factory Act, villagers were working fourteen-hour days and six-day weeks by the age of eight, and could expect that to be the pattern of their whole lives. It took an unusual mind to see this building as the gateway to a world waiting to be explored. But the boy going about his work with Ruddiman's *Rudiments of the Latin Tongue* balanced on the spinning jenny, ignoring both the thunderous racket of the machines and the girls throwing bobbins to try to knock his book off, must have seemed something more than the usual. If one characteristic governed David Livingstone's life, it was independence, and it did so from the start.

David started work in Blantyre mill at the relatively advanced age of ten. Before then, as well as attending the village school, he had worked occasionally herding cows for a local farmer, and clearly had the same attitude to that job: the farmer later recalled, "I didna' think muckle o' that David Livingston when he worked wi' me. He was aye lyin' on his belly readin' a book."

In the mill, David was a piecer, which meant his job was to watch for broken threads and tie them. It required constant attention, making it remarkably indulgent if the management regularly allowed him to read at the loom. (He recalled doing so a good deal later in life.) Monteith & Co. were proud of their health and safety record: only two out of 520 workers died in the first four years the mill was open. The mill was hot, crowded and noisy, the air full of cotton dust and the stink of the toilets, which were tubs emptied once a day, but the workforce was largely free from industrial injuries and disorders.

"Living in one of the 'fairy neuks [nooks]' of creation," says an 1835 national report about the Blantyre villagers, "religious and moral, well fed and clothed, and not overwrought, they seem peculiarly happy, as they ought to be." Co-authored by the manager of the mill, the assessment risks a certain degree of overstatement, but life was far better for the Livingstones than it was in most British mill towns. Far from being allowed to study Latin, it was not unusual for young children to be punched, lashed, tied up and flogged, even dropped head-first into water, for getting drowsy in a fourteen-hour night shift. Monteith & Co. were also uncommonly generous in letting the Livingstone family live in company accommodation, despite the fact that David's father Neil did not work for them. They had a one-room apartment in the block called Shuttle Row, which still stands today, outliving the mill itself thanks to its most famous resident. The family of seven, three boys and two girls, slept, cooked and ate all meals in this room, sharing one washroom with the other twenty-three households of Shuttle Row.

The mill also offered a better life than rural Scotland, where the family had come from. David's grandfather, also Neil Livingstone, had left the small rocky island of Ulva off the coast of Mull, where generations had eked out a living as subsistence farmers, to work in the new mill. He and thousands like him, like those in developing countries today moving from villages to sweatshops, chose the gruelling and exploitative life of waged labour over the even more gruelling existence of subsistence farming.

David's father Neil had started out working in the mill, first as a clerk, then apprenticed to the firm's tailor, David Hunter, a post that came with an education subsidised by the company. Neil married Agnes Hunter, David's daughter, in 1810. The Hunters were from a similar background to the Livingstones, but they were Lowlanders. Keenly evangelical, Neil quit tailoring to become a travelling tea salesman, which allowed him to distribute evangelistic tracts around the region.

David Livingstone had little interest in recording his personal history for posterity, less still his inner life. Much of the information we have about his first twenty-five years is anecdotal and probably influenced by his later career, and it could easily be assembled in a different order with a different interpretation. But he did write very briefly about his childhood impressions of his family, and, whether or not they give us reliable information about the people themselves, they tell us something about how he saw his background. His greatest pride was in the family's honesty. He praised his father's "unflinching honesty", and said that Grandfather Livingstone knew the lives of his own ancestors going back six generations, could find no hint of deceit among any of them, and urged his children to maintain the standard. There are different kinds of honesty, and the kind that makes people admit their failings, concede when they are in the wrong, and tell a story straight however badly it may suit their ends, was presumably not what Livingstone had in mind, as he had very little of it.

He was also proud of his parents' piety, hard work and poverty. Livingstone talked at the height of his career of "my own order, the honest poor", and wrote an epitaph for his mother and father expressing "the thankfulness to God of their children … for poor and pious parents".

When David was thirteen, evening classes in Latin were started by the local teacher, the inauspiciously named Mr McSkimming, subsidised by Monteith & Co. So David worked at the mill from 6 a.m. to 8 p.m., he says, had lessons from 8 p.m. till 10 p.m., and then in his own time studied until midnight – "if my mother did not interfere by jumping up and snatching the books out of my hands". Gradually all the other boys dropped out of the Latin class, and McSkimming was reluctant to spend his time on a single pupil who had no likely use for the language, so he stopped the lessons and David continued to teach himself. He read science and travel books as well as Virgil and Horace, everything he could lay his hands on except novels, of which evangelicals such as his parents generally disapproved, and theology, which David found boring. Other boys at the mill, he recalled in later life, often told him they thought he should go easy on the books, to which he replied, "You think! I can think and act for myself; I don't need anybody to think for me."

It comes as something of a relief to hear of David behaving more like a normal boy. He poached salmon with his elder brother John and younger brother Charles, and it was said that they once smuggled one home in Charles's trousers, Charles receiving sympathy from the villagers for his swollen leg. The three boys took long walks through the surrounding countryside, though for David at least this was, more than anything, another opportunity for learning, as he collected plants and shells to identify and classify. Charles often came back crying from hunger and tiredness, we are told, but always insisted on joining the next expedition. Biographers have been puzzled as to how David, working a fourteen-hour day in the mill, then studying till midnight, every day except the Sabbath, found time for anything else at all, let alone long walks. One answer is that what David in later life called fourteen hours' work, his father, much nearer the time, called twelve hours. Another is that, either way, his story is extraordinary enough if that self-imposed timetable was one he frequently kept to, without assuming that he followed it perpetually or without exception.

David's independence was nowhere more evident than in his spiritual life. At the age of twelve, he had a spiritual crisis, being struck with a sense of how seriously God takes sin, and how appallingly wicked he was in God's sight. The only escape he could see from this predicament was for the Holy Spirit to put him right, and all he could do was wait for that to happen. He waited and waited in terrible anxiety, often in tears, but never talked to anyone about it. The anxiety subsided, but he spent all his teenage years in "a perpetual uneasiness, a soreness of heart … which no amusement or pursuit could assuage". Similarly, when Neil decided to leave the parish church and take the family to Hamilton Congregational Church, David alone refused to come. Even when he did leave the "Auld Kirk", it was not to follow his family, but to join the Relief Church because of its excellent library.

David also rebelled against his father in his reading. Neil was one of those Christians who feared that science was incompatible with religion, especially because of what geologists were discovering about the age of the earth. Neil tried to dissuade David from reading science, or in fact anything other than religious books, and David refused to obey. He did not deny that science and religion were in conflict, but he could not give up his science and so held the two in uncomfortable tension. He refused Neil's instruction to read William Wilberforce's celebrated introduction to evangelical faith, *Practical Christianity*, and was caned for it.

Eventually, however, David's independent path brought him back round to the fold. In the library of the Relief Church, he came at the age of eighteen across a couple of books by Thomas Dick, a defrocked clergyman, theologian and astronomer. Dick argued that not only was studying God's creation scientifically compatible with believing in God, but science was a branch of theology and a form of worship, which made scientists better able to appreciate and understand the ways of God. David was reassured that science and faith did not have to be enemies, and also found the answer to his lonely anxiety about sinfulness. Dick's thoughts on what science reveals about the afterlife made the prospects of heaven and hell more intensely real for David, but at the same time he grasped for the first time the evangelical idea that all a Christian can or need do is to accept Christ's death as a sacrifice for his or her own sin. "[I] cast myself on the mercy of God through Christ," said Livingstone. "A peace and joy entered my heart, to which till then I had been an entire stranger." Elsewhere he likened the change to being cured of colour blindness – what he had learned was not just a revelation in itself but changed the way he saw everything.

David finally joined the rest of his family at Hamilton Congregational Church and applied for membership. It took five months of weeknight classes in Hamilton before the elders agreed he was doctrinally sound enough for the church. The irony is that though he was too independent to follow his family there until then, he found Congregationalism the perfect fit for his personality because of the complete independence of every congregation.

Chapter 2

MISSION

Evangelical conversion was not about the fate of his soul for David Livingstone, but about the purpose of his life. As he put it, "In the glow of love which Christianity inspires, I soon resolved to devote my life to the alleviation of human misery."

The way he wanted to do that, from the start, was overseas mission. This was an endeavour in its early days for the British churches, but it had become a vigorous movement, and both Neil and David, like many Christians, avidly read of the evangelists' exploits. The new wave of mission was led by William Carey, the Northamptonshire shoemaker who took his family to British India in 1793, supported by his Baptist Missionary Society, and opposed by the East India Company. Carey and the Anglican chaplain Henry Martyn translated the Bible into numerous languages and founded a university in Serampore, as well as preaching.

Carey's expedition was the trigger for an extraordinary explosion of foreign mission, and most of the British missionary organizations that reached across the Victorian empire began in the same decade: Carey's Baptist Missionary Society, the interdenominational London Missionary Society (LMS), the Anglican evangelical Church Missionary Society, and on a smaller scale, the Edinburgh Missionary Society and the Glasgow Society for Foreign Missions were all founded between 1792 and 1799.

The LMS had had great success in the south Pacific after sending seventeen agents to Tahiti in 1796. It achieved the remarkable feat of getting a missionary into China, which was strictly closed to the West: Robert Morrison was employed in Canton as a translator for the East India Company from 1809, translated the Bible, and converted eleven people. Non-conformist missionaries in general got good responses preaching to slaves in the British Caribbean, despite violent opposition from their owners. The CMS found it harder to recruit missionaries, and concentrated on sending German Lutherans to former slaves in British Sierra Leone. The Lutherans turned their townships into Christian communities, and founded a thriving college, but suffered a very high death rate from tropical disease. Various unsuccessful expeditions went to Siberia, Ceylon and Egypt.

The most significant for our story was the LMS work in South Africa, which the British had taken from the Dutch (twice) in the French Revolutionary War. Three LMS men arrived there in 1799, including the 51-year-old Dutch doctor Johannes van der Kemp. He defended the Xhosa and Khoikhoi from the Dutch colonists, whom he further annoyed by marrying a former slave. His political stance was maintained by John Philip, who came in 1820, and whose success in promoting black rights with the British governor helped to inspire the Dutch Great Trek out of British territory. The third influential missionary in South Africa was Robert Moffat, who with his wife founded the town of Kuruman beyond the colonial border and translated Christian scriptures into Tswana.

The emergence of the British missionary movement in the 1790s, transforming the work of a few individuals into a national endeavour, is so sudden as to demand explanation. One reason is the progress of the evangelical movement. Carey went to India in the year that John Wesley died, in whose lifetime evangelicalism had moved from the terrifyingly radical fringe into national life so successfully that believers now had the resources, influence and self-confidence to start worrying about the souls of heathens overseas as well as those in Britain.

At the same time, this was a significant period in the self-confidence of the British people. The navy gave Britain an unrivalled global reach commercially and militarily. Though losing America had been traumatic, the growth of British India was already making up for it, with the help of the Caribbean plantations. While the new penal colony of Botany Bay was not commercially or strategically important, it was a bold demonstration of the ease and confidence with which the British made themselves at home on the opposite side of the world. And once they were sending their soldiers, traders, farmers and convicts all over the earth, it was, for those who took their faith seriously, about time they sent their gospel too.

Livingstone had no thoughts of going abroad himself as yet, but resolved "that he would give to the cause of missions all that he might earn beyond what was required for his subsistence." He was helped in this plan when, at eighteen, he was promoted at the mill from piecer to spinner, working the spinning jenny. It was tough work, especially for a "slim, loose-jointed lad", but it allowed him to save money for further study as well as for giving.

Three years later, in 1834, Neil brought home from church a new book which seized David's imagination. *Journal of Three Voyages Along the Coast of China* was by Karl Gützlaff, a Prussian missionary to the Chinese, described by a modern scholar, Arthur Waley, as "a cross between parson and pirate". Unable to settle in China itself, Gützlaff had preached to Chinese expatriates in the Riau Archipelago and Bangkok, before sailing the Chinese coast with opium smugglers. (Not surprisingly, despite its repeated denunciations of Chinese opium addicts, the *Journal* did not mention this travel arrangement.) Wherever he went, Gützlaff distributed Christian literature and medicines. The book was introduced with a rousing essay by William Ellis, an LMS missionary to Polynesia. Altogether, the volume presented China as a vast country of enormous potential, but tyrannical and barbaric, debilitated by superstition, idolatry, poverty and drugs, and where, despite official obstruction, the people eagerly seized Christian writings in their own language, especially when accompanied by medical aid. "A mighty deliverance yet awaits these victims of delusion," declared Ellis, while Gützlaff argued: "There is something irresistible in that holy ardour which counts all things nothing for Christ … I am convinced that individual Christians, thoroughly penetrated with such sentiments, could accomplish more for the benefit of China, than the greatest statesmen."

Reading this, Livingstone heard the call of the Lord. He would not merely support the cause from his little income, he would train in medicine and then go to China as a missionary doctor. He would not join any of the missionary societies, he decided, but would follow his own path, completing his education and medical training before he consulted anyone.

When David first told Neil he planned to go to medical school, they once again found themselves in vehement opposition, Neil apparently feeling that it smacked of worldly ambition. Only later did David explain that it would be for the purposes of evangelism, and then Neil heartily supported his son. The lack of communication here is startling, but again this introduces one of the recurrent themes of Livingstone's life.

David's sights were set on Anderson's University in Glasgow, but with college fees of £12 a year he had to work for another two years to save sufficient funds to start, and then he had to work throughout the six-month vacation. He enrolled at Anderson's in October 1836, he and his father walking the eight miles together through snow. They had a list of recommended lodgings, but they were all too expensive. They eventually found a cheap place in Rottenrow, but David had to move when he found that the landlady stole his tea and sugar.

As well as the requisite anatomy, surgery, physiology, pharmacology and chemistry, David took extra classes in maths, Greek and theology. He impressed his teachers and in several cases made lifelong friends of them. James Young, the lab technician for the Professor of Chemistry, called Livingstone "the best man I ever knew", and Livingstone returned the compliment by naming a river in Africa after him. Under Young's supervision, Livingstone and a fellow pupil, Lyon Playfair, made a new galvanic battery, which the college put on display. Both Playfair and Young went on to lucrative careers in chemistry, the former gaining a seat in the House of Lords and the latter becoming a millionaire through paraffin. Such were the possible futures that beckoned a young man of such application as David Livingstone. More modestly, his landlord, Mr Dove, offered him a teaching post worth £150 a year; "David," reported his father, "said he was grateful for his kindness, but that was not the object on which he had set his heart."

David felt homesick living on his own in Glasgow, but rationed himself to one home visit each month to start with. According to his sister Janet, this was because two medical students from Blantyre who had gone to Glasgow University returned home every weekend and then found themselves suspected of body snatching. After some months of this, David decided the danger was past and started walking home every Saturday morning. Fergus Ferguson, a draper from Hamilton Church who drove a cart into the city each Monday, offered him a lift whenever he wanted one, but he would have missed the first lecture, so he walked every week, whatever the weather.

He completed his first-year exams in April 1837. As a further example of enlightened capitalism, Monteith & Co. had kept his job open during his first year at college, and though Neil wanted him to take a short break, David started at the mill the following morning. He was already struggling financially, however, and had to borrow money from his elder brother, John, who now supported a family, to pay for his second year's expenses. Reluctantly, David decided to apply to join the London Missionary Society, and take their funding.

The society does not seem to have been particularly impressed by David's application. He was after all a 24-year-old factory hand with no useful experience and an incomplete education. His minister at Hamilton wrote to Mission House introducing him to the directors in August, and on 5 September 1837 David wrote to them telling his story and describing his faith. He had to wait until January 1838 for a reply, which presented him with their standard questionnaire about beliefs, spiritual life, church experience, health and employment. Asked "What do you apprehend are the proper duties of a Christian missionary?", Livingstone answered:

> *His duties chiefly are, I apprehend, to endeavour by*
> *every means in his power to make known the Gospel*
> *by preaching, exhortation, conversation, instruction*
> *of the young; improving, so far as in his power, the*
> *temporal condition of those among whom he labours,*
> *by introducing the arts and sciences of civilization,*
> *and doing everything in his power to commend*
> *Christianity to their hearts and consciences.* [1]

The philanthropy here is Livingstone's own concern and not anything that he would have found in the LMS's own publications. His statement also exemplifies what to modern ears is the alarm bell-ringing language of imperialistic arrogance, the desire to bring "civilization" to the dark continent – although stripped of the politically incorrect language there is nothing there that necessarily goes beyond what Western agencies and governments today call "development".

Asked about marriage, he replied comprehensively and fervently:

> *Unmarried; under no engagement relating to*
> *marriage, never made proposals of marriage, nor*
> *conducted myself so to any woman as to cause her*
> *to suspect that I intended anything relating to*

> *marriage; and, so far as my present wishes are*
> *concerned, I should prefer going out unmarried, that*
> *I might be without that care which the concerns of a*
> *family necessarily induce, and give myself wholly to*
> *the work.* [2]

His resolution would have pleased St Paul, but in fact the LMS preferred missionaries to be married.

Again the LMS directors showed no undue haste, and Livingstone had still not heard from them by Easter, the end of his second year at Anderson's, which turned out to be a crisis point for him. First, in the closing weeks of term he was so ill that Neil came to visit and asked, "As you are very ill I would like to know if your mind is at rest."

"I am so weak I can scarcely think," replied David, "but I am resting on 'I will never leave thee nor forsake thee'."

"That's enough," said Neil. "If anything happened I just wanted your mother and me to be satisfied." He took David home in a hired vehicle, and Agnes sat up three nights with him, but he recovered in time for his exams.

Then, when he returned to work at the mill, the manager told him he would not keep holding the job open for him if he went back to college in the autumn. This made the fact that he had still heard nothing from the LMS alarming, so Neil secretly wrote to them in April 1838. He told them about the discipline, sacrifice and success with which David had applied himself to his studies, and argued that any suspicion that he was turning to mission merely to escape drudgery was disproved by his refusal of the teaching post offered by his landlord. The society eventually wrote in August offering David an interview. He had a second interview the following month, and was accepted on probation.

Chapter 3

JOINING UP

To start his training, Livingstone was sent to Chipping Ongar in Essex with six other probationers, for a three-month course in theology and ancient languages taught by Revd Richard Cecil. Among the students, he got on especially well with Joseph Moore, who recalled, "I grew daily more attached to him. If I were asked why, I should be rather at a loss to reply. There was a truly indescribable charm about him which, with all his rather ungainly ways and by no means winning face, attracted almost everyone." Another classmate, Walter Inglis, agreed that he was not good looking: "I have to admit he was 'no bonny'. His face wore at all times the strongly marked lines of potent will."

Livingstone and Moore both struggled as theology students. Cecil complained about Livingstone's "heaviness of manner, united as it is with a rusticity, not likely to be removed". Students had to preach and lead prayers in local churches, and for no readily apparent reason Cecil made them write their sermons, learn them by heart and then recite them without notes. Livingstone performed poorly, his preaching mechanical and his prayers hesitant. Once, at Stanford Rivers, Livingstone was delivering his sermon when his mind went blank: "Friends," he said, "I have forgotten all I had to say," and he fled the building.

At the end of three months, in December 1838, the LMS examined and was ready to fail both of them, Moore said, until one of the directors persuaded the board to extend the probation. The pair were sent back to Ongar as "naughty boy[s]".

It took another six months before the directors were satisfied. Late in January 1839, Cecil reported that Livingstone's problems continued as ever, "but he has sense and quiet vigour; his temper is good and his character substantial, so that I do not like the thought of his being rejected".

The timetable at Ongar was more relaxed than Livingstone was used to, and left him plenty of time for country rambles. He sometimes took a young local boy, Isaac Taylor, with him, who recalled the excursions forty years later: "I remember his step, the characteristic forward tread, firm, simple, resolute, neither fast nor slow, no hurry and no dawdle, but which evidently meant – getting there." He also had time for an inconclusive romantic foray. He fell for Catherine Ridley, a local merchant's daughter. They exchanged books and poems, but David found himself ill prepared to deal with "those who have been ladies all their lives", and during his whole time at Ongar he never told her his feelings.

During this time, Livingstone made a momentous change of plan: instead of China, he would go to South Africa. Where this decision came from is not clear. It has often been said that it was from meeting the LMS missionary Robert Moffat on leave from South Africa, because that is how Moffat remembered it himself forty years later. These meetings, though, happened when Livingstone was living in London in 1840, and as we shall see, he was already bound for Africa by then, so they can only have reaffirmed his redirection. Livingstone himself, writing in 1857, described the change of plan thus:

> ... *there being no prospect of an early peace with the Chinese, and as another inviting field was opening out through the labors of Mr. Moffat, I was induced to turn my thoughts to Africa.* [3]

Like Moffat's recollection, this seems to place the decision after the start of the First Opium War in 1840, but as we shall see, several letters at the time show that he had already changed direction by 1839. Livingstone clearly misremembered.

How exactly Livingstone's plans were changed is unclear then, but the likelihood is that the decision came first from the LMS directors. It was their prerogative, and when John Moir, the minister at Hamilton, visited them in May 1839 to hear about Livingstone's progress and suggested that India would be the place for him, he was told "they did not think that his gifts fitted him for India, and that Africa would be a more suitable field". Perhaps the directors felt that Livingstone's Scottish rusticity was better suited to the less sophisticated society of southern Africans than that of the Chinese or Indians. This would also explain why Livingstone misattributed the change of plan to the Opium War: his memory was at its worst when the truth was embarrassing.

When the directors finally approved Livingstone in June, he was dismayed to hear they had changed their minds again and were sending him neither to Africa, China nor India, but to the British Caribbean and its population of former slaves. He was to go straightaway. Livingstone saw all his plans for medical mission foundering. The Caribbean islands had plenty of doctors, so he would be redundant and they would see him as an upstart who threatened their livelihood and they might take any chance to spoil his reputation. Moreover, going now he would have no chance to complete his medical training. He would not be a missionary doctor after all, he felt, but a mere colonial local minister.

Livingstone wrote to the directors on 2 July 1839, saying Cecil had told him "that I should be employed in the West Indies in preference to South Africa", and humbly protesting that while his only ambition was to spread the gospel, going to the West Indies would waste the incredible effort he had made to learn science. Cannily, Livingstone also said that, though he had finally been passed by them, he felt the need for more LMS education before he was fit for mission, and wanted to spend the rest of the year being taught by Richard Cecil before completing his medical training. The directors agreed to all his requests: he would restart his medical training in London in the new year, "to fit himself for some station in South Africa or the South Seas".

On 2 January 1840, Livingstone moved to the LMS boarding house run by Margaret Sewell at 57 Aldersgate Street in London, and then enrolled at the British and Foreign Medical School. His training so far having only been theoretical, he gained clinical experience at Charing Cross, Moorfields Eye Hospital and the General Dispensary in Aldersgate Street. He also retook anatomy at the Hunterian Museum, despite having successfully completed the subject at Anderson's. He wanted not just to qualify that year, but to seize all the knowledge available. He also tried to continue preaching every Sunday, but soon gave up, disappointing nobody.

It was at this time that Livingstone met Robert Moffat. While he studied, the celebrated LMS missionary was touring Britain on furlough from South Africa, where he and his wife Mary had now been for twenty years. They promoted the mission with their stories, recuperated, and printed a Tswana New Testament. Robert visited the Aldersgate boarding house, and forty years later, he remembered meeting Livingstone thus:

> *I observed soon that this young man was interested in my story, that he would sometimes come quietly and ask me a question or two, and that he was always desirous to know where I was to speak in public, and attended on these occasions. By and by he asked me whether I thought he would do for Africa. I said I believed he would, if he would not go to an old station, but would advance to unoccupied ground, specifying the vast plain to the north, where I had sometimes seen, in the morning sun, the smoke of a thousand villages, where no missionary had ever*

> *been. At last Livingstone said: "What is the use of my*
> *waiting for the end of this abominable opium war? I*
> *will go at once to Africa."*[4]

Though the last sentence is misremembered, clearly Moffat's stories of Africa captured Livingstone's imagination in the way that Gützlaff's stories of China had done. Perhaps, learning later that he had originally been bound for China, Moffat leapt to the pleasant assumption that he himself had changed Livingstone's course. Moffat told Livingstone exciting stories of his successful mission, but also warned him there were serious obstacles, even in the form of the celebrated John Philip, superintendent of the LMS South Africa mission, who he said had become autocratic and senile, and had been diverted into local politics.

Further inspiration came from the rally that Livingstone attended at Exeter Hall on the Strand on 1 June 1840, to mark the first anniversary of the Society for the Extinction of the Slave Trade and for the Civilization of Africa. While Britain had abolished its own slave trade in 1807, and persuaded other countries, such as France and Portugal, to pass similar acts, the latter were less interested in effectively suppressing the trade, so it had continued to grow.

Prince Albert was president and brought with him a dizzying number of the most powerful men in Britain as well as anti-slavery veterans. The Society's leader was Thomas Fowell Buxton, the MP anointed by Wilberforce to continue his fight against slavery, and arguably the person most responsible for the 1833 Emancipation Act. He was also influentially concerned with the treatment of indigenous people in South Africa.

Buxton was a thrilling public speaker, and he told his audience that since abolishing its own slave trade, the British had spent more than £16m in suppressing the international trade – in which time the number of Africans sold into slavery each year had doubled. The remedies which Buxton

proposed were Christianity, commerce and "civilization".
As abolitionists had long argued, to stop the trade they had
to stop African dependence on it, by what today one would
call development: agriculture, industry, legitimate trade with
Europe and America, writing, science, medicine, plus religious
education. The society was not meant to engage directly in any
of these, but to promote them, and to discover and disseminate
relevant information – starting with a government-sponsored
expedition up the Niger. Buxton summed up the aim: "to
arrest the destruction of mankind; to pour a blessing upon a
continent in ruins; to send civilization and the mild truths of
the Gospel over a region, in comparison with which Britain
herself is but a speck upon the ocean."

The meeting was important for Livingstone, despite the fact
that the expedition was a failure, and that he himself was going
to a part of Africa the slave trade had never reached. It meant that
when, disillusioned by his own failure as an evangelist, he went
into regions the slave trade was also entering, he had a ready-
made strategy: to use commercial development to attack the
slave trade and advance Christian mission, and seize the chance
to play a crucial part in bringing the mission of Wilberforce and
Buxton to its eventual fulfilment.

Livingstone's workload was so terrific that he was trying at
one point to get by on four hours' sleep. He fell seriously ill
and was sent home to Glasgow. Moore, who put him on the
boat, feared he was dying, but he returned to his studies within
the month.

When he finally completed his course in November 1840, he
was distressed to find that he would not be able to take the
Royal College of Surgeons' exams, because the LMS would
not pay the fee. He comforted himself with the thought that "I
shall be able to practise medicine amongst the Bechuana as well
without as with the licence of the Royal College of Physicians",
but in the end the directors agreed to pay for him to sit the

equivalent exams in Glasgow, which were much cheaper. He stayed at Blantyre for one night before returning. His sister Janet recalled:

> *On the morning of the 17th of November, we got up*
> *at 5 o'clock. My mother made coffee. David read the*
> *121st and 135th Psalms, and prayed. My father and*
> *he walked to Glasgow to catch the Liverpool steamer.* [5]

Livingstone was ordained on 20 November, and then on 8 December, on the sailing ship *George*, he left London for the Cape of Good Hope. His instructions were to go to Moffat's Kuruman settlement to learn the ropes and the language, and then, when Moffat returned from England, to establish his own permanent mission station up to a hundred miles north. The way Livingstone's career actually went is different enough to make one wonder whether he ever had any intention of doing that at all.

Livingstone in Southern Africa
1841–1853

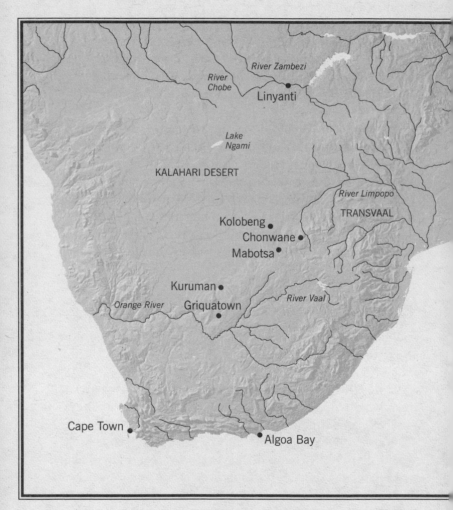

Chapter 4

A NEW WORLD

Livingstone was completely unprepared for the experience of being on a small sailing ship in the Atlantic, his sea journeys until then being in steamers around British coastal waters. For a thousand miles the journey was increasingly stormy, until the vessel, in Livingstone's words, "writhed and twisted about terribly. Imagine if you can a ship in a fit of epilepsy." The passengers' trunks broke out of their ropes and were thrown about the cabins. Livingstone remained calm, and watched the horror of his fellow LMS missionaries, the Scottish couple Mr and Mrs Ross, with disdain – that at least is how he remembered it.

They enjoyed a quiet stretch in west African waters, but then a worse storm than ever off Cape Verde drove the ship west and split the foremast. If they pressed on towards South Africa, Captain Donaldson reckoned, the next gale would destroy the mast, and they would run out of water a month before they could expect to reach land, so they headed for the nearest port where the mast could be repaired, which was Rio de Janeiro, four days south-west.

As the Rosses did not want to see the city, Livingstone disembarked alone, finding it "certainly the finest place I ever saw". He loved the cathedral, declaring that if he could ever abandon Congregationalism for the established church, he would skip Presbyterianism and Anglicanism and go straight to Catholicism. But he was appalled by the drunken brawls of British and US sailors, and visited the most violent bar he could find to hand out tracts. As if he couldn't wait to head into uncharted Africa, he ignored warnings about passing the city limits, went into the forest, had dinner with a family he found living there and took a shower under a waterfall.

The fourteen-week voyage was not a time-killing exercise for Livingstone. He studied Dutch and learned what Tswana he could from Moffat's New Testament, and he persuaded the captain to teach him navigation, staying up into the night making lunar observations with him. As Livingstone was expected to found a new mission station and stay there permanently, navigation was not an obviously necessary skill. Perhaps he learned it for the sheer love of knowledge and it proved invaluable to his later career by mere chance, or perhaps he already had a secret hope that his adventures in Africa would go beyond his job description.

His relations with fellow missionaries were less cordial. The Rosses were newlyweds, an odd pair, Livingstone thought, and too proud of each other. William Ross praised the advantages of marriage with what felt like insufferable smugness, reminding Livingstone that Mary Moffat had urged him to marry, and quoting the verse "Two are better than one". He then, apparently, accused Livingstone of trying to seduce his wife when treating her for seasickness. "I was conscious of just as little inclination towards his wife," Livingstone said, "as I now have towards my grandmother's cat." Livingstone quickly conceived an immovable contempt for the couple, and when he found them both having to throw up into one bowl was delighted to remind William, "Two are better than one." It was hardly a good augury for Livingstone's career or a good advertisement for his character that by the time he reached Africa his first two colleagues were already his enemies, but as augury or advertisement it was perfectly accurate.

Livingstone came to Africa with some fixed ideas about his job. One was the importance of what he called "native agency": as the LMS directors had agreed, the best missionaries in Africa would be Africans, so it was his job not just to convert them but to train them for the work, as many as possible as soon as possible. "Native agency", he wrote to a friend in Hamilton, "… is the only thing that can evangelise the world." Another passionate idea was that he was not there to support or continue the work of any other missionary. He saw himself as a pioneer, pushing forward the frontier of the gospel. Again, the LMS directors had agreed that his mission was to reach new tribes in "the Interior", but his ambition went beyond that: as he wrote to his family, "I would never build on another man's foundation. I shall preach the gospel beyond every other man's line of things."

This phrase offers a revealing glimpse of the mix of Livingstone's motives in going to South Africa. His commitment to evangelism and desire to be of use to the Christian cause were evident, as were his humanitarian impulses; but alongside them there is clearly a sizeable measure of ego, the desire to be not merely effective but magnificent. Throughout his career, it often seemed that he was driven by mixed motives – these and more – but it was rarely clear which had the upper hand, and almost certainly not clear to Livingstone himself.

Arriving in Cape Town on 15 March 1841, Livingstone was happily surprised to find that the allegations Moffat had made about Philip seemed quite unfounded. Far from being autocratic and senile, the mission superintendent turned out to be humble and competent; and rather than overly political, Livingstone discovered he had saved native peoples, especially the Khoikhoi (or Hottentots), from slavery at the hands of the Boers. Philip had worked with Thomas Fowell Buxton to persuade the colonial secretary at Westminster to extend full civil rights to non-white people of the Cape Colony and the whole British Empire. Philip arranged treaties between the colony and neighbouring peoples, and testified to Buxton's parliamentary committee on aborigines, which returned territory the British had seized from the Xhosa.

But Philip, after clearing his name with Livingstone, made his own accusations against Moffat. He told Livingstone Moffat was divisive, turning his friends at Kuruman against the missionaries at Griquatown – the one other LMS settlement outside the colonial boundary – and both against the missionaries in the Cape Colony. He said that Moffat was behind plans to set up a regional committee that would govern all missionaries beyond the colony (though in truth it came from the directors), which appalled the ardently self-sufficient Livingstone.

Livingstone was dismayed by these political divisions, denouncing them as a disgrace. While doing so, he took sides as belligerently as anyone, turning against the Moffats. In fact, Livingstone would turn out to be about as quarrelsome as any missionary in Africa.

Livingstone was also saddened by the lack of pioneering spirit among his colleagues in the Cape. With all Africa stretching out before them, there were British villages around the port hoarding three ministers. "I cannot help thinking," he wrote to a friend, "that the poor Christians in England [who donate to the LMS] are defrauded by such English people in these towns... who detain missionaries amongst them." He was determined that his own ventures should put their timidity to shame.

The eleven-week journey to the Kuruman mission station was a delight for Livingstone, apart from the fact that he was accompanied by Mr and Mrs Ross. They sailed 450 miles east to Algoa Bay, and then travelled a much slower 550 miles north by ox-drawn wagons filled with furniture, crockery, clothes and supplies, led by African drivers. The grassy land of the coast became increasingly barren and alien, turning into rocky, thorny desert, with almost impassable dried river valleys. But the young naturalist, who loved his rambles around Lanarkshire and Kent, was thrilled to see scorpions, giraffes, wildebeest, springbok and many other new creatures. For the first time in his life he felt free: they were their own masters, camping, eating and hunting where and when they wanted.

Livingstone fell in love with this new world, austere as it sometimes was. If, as we have seen, there were elements of both ego and altruism in his desire to extend Christian mission into unmapped territory, another powerful motive was the sheer love of exploration. Even now, before he had reached Kuruman for the first time, this fledgling missionary was already talking about taking a trip 500 miles further north, not to preach to Africans but to "discover" Lake Ngami, which no European had seen. "There is an anxiety amongst all the missionaries to do something," Livingstone wrote to a friend. "Every one would like to see it." He had heard that Moffat planned an expedition, and that the French missionaries planned to beat him to it. "If they give your humble servant a month or two to acquire the colloquial language they may spare themselves the pain of being first 'in at the death'." There was a slim evangelistic rationale for such an expedition: geographical discoveries were tremendously popular with the British public, and if a missionary society could claim responsibility and publish the account, it would enhance its reputation and its income. But it is fair to say that Livingstone's comments reflect more personal ambition than concern for corporate PR.

They visited several Christian villages en route to Kuruman, all outstations of Moffat's rivals at Griquatown. Livingstone was impressed. Having been shocked during his journey to see naked men covered in red paint and brandishing weapons, he found these Christians properly dressed, and so well versed in the faith that he and the Rosses got a telling-off for travelling on a Sunday. (Unusually for an evangelical, Livingstone did not believe in the Sabbath, considering it an Old Testament law superseded by Christ. He "looks on Sabbath observance in its English acceptation as a day of one's life lost", as his friend John Kirk would later say; but he agreed to preach the practice to Africans in order to present a united Christian tradition.) Livingstone's belief in "native agency" was reinforced by the fact that the only permanent preachers in these villages were Tswana converts. Livingstone had brought copies of Moffat's

Tswana New Testament and sold many, saying, "I never saw such thirst for the word of God before."

Livingstone's relationship with the Rosses only worsened during the journey. "He and I are not on good terms," Livingstone wrote to a friend, "because I speak out, and pay no more regard to his opinions on the ground of his education (his wife's boast) than if he were a Hottentot boy and could not read." When Livingstone needed academic advice, he preferred to write to a friend in India, because Ross "has such a precious idea of his extensive learning that I have not heart to ask him". Livingstone now even considered the Rosses' admiration for Moffat as evidence of their silliness.

They reached Kuruman on 31 July 1841. It has been claimed that Livingstone was bitterly disappointed by the Christian mission there, how few people had been converted and how poor their Christianity was, and that he considered Moffat a fraud because of the claims he had made for it. This is a rather over-imaginative reconstruction of his feelings, considering that his actual words were nothing but praise. A large proportion of the population were believers, he reported to the directors, and "the contrast between what they were and have now become is most striking". In the Moffats' absence, the mission was run by the "artisan missionaries" (i.e. laypeople sent for their practical skills): 61-year-old Robert Hamilton and Rogers Edwards and his wife, who in their own reports, Livingstone said, "have if anything understated their achievements". Mrs Edwards' Sunday school was particularly fruitful. "While I magnify the grace manifested both in and by them," Livingstone concluded, "I pray to be enabled to walk with humility and zeal in their footsteps."

There was just one thing about Kuruman that disappointed Livingstone: it was a single village in the middle of a vast empty wilderness. He had pictured it as something of a Christian metropolis, and a gateway to the north, to those "thousand villages, where no missionary had ever been". Instead, the village had a population of less than a thousand, of whom 350 came to church and forty were baptized. Kuruman itself was lush and green, thanks to Moffat's irrigation and cultivation, but "all around is a dreary desert", with nothing for miles but "low stunted scraggy bushes, many of them armed with bent thorns villainously sharp and strong". Only another thousand people lived within a ten-mile circle, and the missionaries found them – and in fact all tribes within a hundred miles – fervently hostile to Christianity.

This was a devastating blow for Livingstone's cherished scheme to march on Africa with an army of African missionaries. There were simply not yet enough African Christians. Livingstone would have to make do with two or three, and take them 250 miles north, where the people had never met Christians, though they had heard about them, and were so far from the prejudices of the tribes near Kuruman that they had sent requests for missionaries.

There were consolations in this disappointing prospect. Not least was that Livingstone had the perfect excuse to disregard his explicit instructions to attach himself to tribes in the vicinity of Kuruman. He wanted to go further into Africa than other missionaries and he wanted to be the first to see Lake Ngami, and the sparsity of the region around Kuruman would give him the opportunity.

And that opportunity came sooner than expected. Rogers Edwards, having worked under Moffat for ten years, now had permission to found his own mission station. Being the only preacher at Kuruman in Moffat's absence he had been waiting for the newcomers to relieve him so he could go on a reconnaissance trip. He suggested one of them hold the fort and the other come with him; both were keen to go, but as Mrs Ross was pregnant the lot fell to the delighted Livingstone.

Describing their plans in a letter to a friend, Livingstone said, "I shall proceed to the northward.... Mr Edwards of this station intends to accompany me...." This is an odd turn of phrase for someone who was joining an expedition that had long been planned by a man with seventeen years' African experience, but as far as Livingstone was concerned he himself had been sent into the interior, so he himself was going, and if Edwards was also going then Edwards was accompanying him. It is a trivial enough point, but Livingstone's attitude was to have very serious consequences.

Before leaving, Livingstone concentrated on learning the Tswana language. He found it a simple one, and any problems he had with it he attributed to the fact that "the natives do jumble their words so together and then they are so stupid at understanding if there is any blunder in my sentences". Then in September 1841, less than two months after arriving in Kuruman, Edwards and Livingstone set off on a 750-mile round trip to the north-east with a couple of African Christians, including Pomare, the son of a *kgosi* or chief, to visit various tribes of the Tswana people.

It was an arduous journey, slow, hot and thirsty. It was midsummer, and Livingstone noted that "the enormous centipedes coming out by mistake from their holes were roasted to death on the ground". Livingstone already wore the sailor's hat that would become his trademark. They visited relatively nearby tribes and confirmed those tribes' scorn for Christianity, which Livingstone reckoned was because of its demand for monogamy. Then for more than a hundred miles they saw no one, just herds of horses, giraffes, ostriches, antelopes and rhinoceroses.

All of these they hunted for food. Livingstone found wild horse as good as beef, but boiled rhinoceros was "toughness itself" and tasted of train oil, though a porridge made the following day from its gravy was better. Reporting the expedition to his family, the one thing he forbade them to repeat was his eating rhino: "it would look as if I meant it to be understood I endured great sufferings." Throughout his life Livingstone had a horror of exaggerating, or at least of being thought to exaggerate, the hardships of his travels. The most unsympathetic accounts of his career have attributed this tendency, when seen in later life, solely to his desire to make Africa seem more attractive to those he wanted to recruit to his colonial ventures, but as it is already in evidence here it was clearly a deeper and more personal inclination.

The first people the travellers met in this region were children of the Bakalihari tribe, a poor desert people who were used as slaves by other Tswana tribes. Livingstone was surprised that children were unsupervised in hyena country while their mothers were up a mountain picking berries. When the women returned, they were too scared to come near at first, but Livingstone gave them some buttons his mother had sent as a gift and a joint of rhino, and they gave him berries in return.

One hundred and fifty miles from Kuruman they found the Bakgatla (or Bakhatla), a medium-sized tribe of about 1,200 people, in a forty-mile valley, which the big game hunter Roualeyn Gordon-Cumming called "one of the most beautiful spots in Africa." The town was fenced with thorn, built around the *kgotla*, a town square for meetings. The houses were made from clay, dung and thatch, and the people dressed in karosses (skins). The tribe were without their chief, Mosealele, and his *bagakolodi* or court, who had escaped into the Kalahari Desert to evade the powerful Zulu king Mzilikazi (or Mosilikatze). The valley was rich in iron ore, and they were the only Tswana tribe who smelted iron – "the Sheffield of the interior" as Livingstone put it – which they used for weapons and needles. Only a few families were involved in the secret process, but Edwards and Livingstone were granted the rare privilege of viewing it, because they had not had sex recently enough to "bewitch" it and burn the iron. Livingstone reckoned that going easier on the leather bellows and adding limestone would have been a more reliable precaution, but they did not take his advice.

The missionaries went north to visit the Bakwena (or Bakwain) and Bangwaketse tribes. At each town, the chief summoned the people into the cattle field for a service, which became known as *pina ea sekoa*, "the white man's dance". The missionaries sat among them and one would preach a one-point sermon, followed by prayer, and conversation with those who wanted to stay for it. Livingstone offered medical aid, and people came from over a hundred miles to see *Ngake*, the healer. He was impressed by their toughness as patients, letting him cut out a tumour, for example, while "they sit and talk as if they felt nothing". He and Edwards were given presents and meals.

As Livingstone had predicted, the missionaries were better received by these tribes than those near Kuruman. Their medicine was an obvious attraction, as were their European goods, especially the guns that they brought for hunting and personal protection. They also mended any guns a chief might already have. The most powerful attraction though was the least obvious: for years the Tswana had been terrorized and woefully depleted of people and livestock by Mzilikazi, until he was defeated and forced north by the Boers, and similarly so-called "Manatee" raiders had been driven away by Griquatown. Consequently, Tswana chiefs hoped they would be safe from such enemies as long as they had a white man living with them. Some people the missionaries visited had seen a white person before: David Hume, the Scottish ivory trader based at Kuruman. But no missionary had been so far north until now.

After they left one village, a twelve-year-old orphan girl caught them up, desperate to escape being sold as a wife, followed by an armed man sent to bring her back. Pomare intervened and negotiated, the girl gave back the beads she wore as her bride price, Livingstone hid her "and though fifty men had come for her, they would not have got her".

Things looked good for their plans. Edwards told the LMS that the Bakgatla offered the best new mission base once the chief had returned, and he waited for their consent. Livingstone cared less for the directors' consent and wanted to get building their houses straightaway, but as a lay missionary Edwards was too insecure about his standing in the organization for such a risk. Livingstone needed Edwards' building skills and had been told by the directors to heed his advice, so he came back to Kuruman with him.

Livingstone felt discouraged that no one had yet responded with any great conviction to their preaching, but the journey confirmed his belief in the need to recruit African missionaries. Seeing Pomare in action, Livingstone realized that he understood and was understood by fellow Tswana people in ways Europeans could hardly hope for. As neither Philip nor Moffat was keen on using African missionaries, Livingstone's letters to the directors constantly urged them to keep supporting the scheme. The sheer vastness of Africa impressed on him the hopelessness of sending Europeans to cover it; even the long slow miles they had themselves crossed amounted to "a mere iota compared to what is yet to be possessed by the missionaries of the cross".

Chapter 5

THE PIONEER

When Edwards and Livingstone returned to Kuruman in December 1841, there was still no sign of Moffat. While Edwards waited for permission to start building with the Bakgatla, Livingstone worked as the Kuruman doctor, treating people who came from miles around. His patience lasted a little more than a month, and then on 10 February 1842 he set off on another trip north-east, without Edwards, taking two Tswana Christians, Pomare and the older Mebalwe Molehane, and two wagon drivers. He explained the trip to the LMS directors saying that it was easier to learn the language with no British people around, that he wanted a break from his medical practice, and that he wanted to put native agents to work.

After twelve days' travel they reached the Bakgatla, and paid the briefest of visits before moving on. Presumably this was because Livingstone wanted to arrange placements for his preachers, and there was no point in doing that where he and Edwards were planning their own mission station, though he gave the directors the extraordinary explanation that the Bakgatla were too far south to be receptive to Christianity.

Livingstone's team then went a hundred miles north to spend a month with the Bakwena. This tribe of about 2,000 people was split under rival chiefs Bube and his nephew Sechele, and Livingstone angered Sechele by choosing Bube's faction to be his hosts. (He had visited both with Edwards.) Bube agreed to have Pomare as a preacher, at Livingstone's expense. Bube also let them set up a school for Pomare to teach in, and attempt irrigation for his garden.

Livingstone told the Bakwena that irrigation was "my way of making rain", far better than their meteorological magic, but it was a risky scheme. He knew nothing about irrigation and had to make it up as he went along; he had not thought ahead, so their only equipment was sharpened sticks, skins, shells and bowls; he could do little work himself after getting badly sunburned on the first day; and he had been told repeatedly that Africans were constitutionally work-shy, because the missionaries had rarely managed to get them to work for wages. But, persuaded that a dam and canal would benefit the whole town, the Bakwena worked very hard – though Livingstone was disgusted to see that the men left the heavy lifting to their wives – and after a tornado and flood destroyed their first two attempts, their project was finally successful.

There was a lot riding on it. In addition to its practical value, the irrigation was a calculated exercise in Christian propaganda. Rain and healing were both the job of the Tswana holy man, and just as Livingstone's medicine was meant to outclass traditional rituals and remedies, so he hoped his waterway would discredit "those impostors called 'Rain Makers'". In fact the rainmakers were as keen on it as anyone. Pomare's placement was less successful, as he contracted malaria and left with Livingstone.

Continuing north towards the Bamangwato (or Bangwato), a tribe of about 1,800 people, they had to abandon their wagon when the going got too sandy, and go fifty miles on foot. They got a very warm welcome, Chief Sekomi giving them rhinoceros meat and a large elephant tusk and inviting them to his mother's house. Sekomi repeatedly warned them about going outside the town alone, because of lions, and Livingstone repeatedly ignored him, believing the Tswana were cowards, until a woman was killed by a lion in her own garden.

Livingstone had his most penetrating conversations so far with the Bamangwato, and he was appalled by what they revealed. As he reported to the directors:

> *The population is sunk in the very lowest state of both mental and moral degradation, so much so indeed it*

*must be difficult or rather impossible for Christians at
home to realise anything like an accurate notion of the
grossness of that darkness that shrouds their minds.* [6]

He found that the Tswana seemed to have no idea of life
after death – an impression that Moffat was at the same time
broadcasting to the British public – and they seemed to find
the subject morbid. Their ideas about God or gods also seemed
"vague and contradictory", their only word for "god" being the
same title they used for their chiefs and for Livingstone himself.

Despite such dire ignorance of Christian truth, the
Bamangwato baffled Livingstone by showing no inclination
to change their minds. He was pleased when Chief Sekomi,
without any prompting from Livingstone at all, said to him,
"I wish you would change my heart. Give me medicine to
change it, for it is proud, proud and angry, angry always." But
when Livingstone explained that such change comes spiritually,
through reading the Bible, Sekomi was unimpressed, insisting,
"Nay I wish to have it changed by medicine." Witchcraft was
central to the Tswana worldview, and so they naturally thought
of the mysterious power of European medicine in the same
terms; for example, pouring it over a child's head if she would
not take it orally, or parents taking it for children, or expecting
it to make them run faster. Livingstone was annoyed by their
failure to differentiate between witchcraft, science and religion.

In fact Livingstone started to feel seriously discouraged by
the lack of response to Christian teaching. As unrealistic as
it may seem to imagine that the whole worldview of African
people could be overthrown in a matter of weeks, that does
seem to have been his expectation, doubtless influenced by
missionary literature from Acts to Gützlaff, and by his sense
of the overwhelmingly obvious superiority of Christian truth
to Tswana superstition. If the Africans who had been preached
to before had failed to accept Christianity, he thought, it was
because of bad experiences of Europeans, so by going further

from the Cape Colony he would be starting almost from scratch, and so could expect more instant success. So the Bamangwato dismayed him more than ever: they had had almost no contact with Europeans and yet still preferred what he saw as the wicked nonsense of their traditions.

Livingstone and his companions (including a bodyguard of thirty supplied by Sekomi) then walked twenty-four-miles to where the Bakaa tribe lived, their 250 huts perched on 700-foot black volcanic rocks, which Livingstone said looked like gigantic pews. His companions told him that he was the third white man to visit the Bakaa, and that they had murdered the second, a trader called Gibson, poisoning him along with his companions for his wagon and ox. This was not the kind of reception to deter Livingstone, so up they went. The Bakaa seemed much less curious to see a white man than other tribes, only the kgosi and two attendants coming to welcome him, which Livingstone interpreted as shame for their crime and fear of retribution. They wore plundered jugs and bits of gun around their necks. However, when Livingstone trustingly ate the chief's porridge and lay down to sleep without fear, they became more friendly, and he told them in broken Tswana of Christ, who had given his life to save his betrayers. All in all it was unfortunate that one of Livingstone's companions took ill while they were there, causing talk of poisoning, but they left on good terms.

Livingstone returned to his wagon and went back to Kuruman in June 1842. Within a year of his arrival, he had been further into Africa than any other missionary. He returned to the work of doctor, preacher, printer and builder alongside the Edwardses, Rosses and Hamilton, but he was immediately restless for his next journey. There were still no instructions from London, nor any sign of Moffat, so he prepared to return straightaway to the Bakwena, but was forestalled by bad news.

The Bangwaketse tribe, led by Chief Sebeque, lived twelve days away from Kuruman and was friendly with the missionaries.

They were attacked and massacred by another nearby tribe who had guns. This was not Mzilikazi's Matabele (or Amandebele) that they so feared – in fact Sebeque's inspired generalship had seen off Mzilikazi's attacks while other Tswana tribes had lost much of their cattle, and it was these tribes who were now replenishing their stock at Sebeque's expense. Livingstone had sent a message to Sebeque at the time, warning him of the danger, but for various reasons Sebeque did not act on the tip off. Tswana Christians from Kuruman were visiting Bangwaketse when the attack happened, and circumstantial evidence made Sebeque believe they had conspired with the attackers. Because of this, no one from Kuruman would leave town with Livingstone, fearing Sebeque would avenge himself on anyone who fell into his hands.

So Livingstone waited until his friends felt Sebeque might have calmed down sufficiently. In the meantime, he helped Edwards build a chapel at a nearby village. Then news reached them that the missionaries of the region were debating whether Edwards as a layman should be allowed to set up his new mission station, or be kept as a manual worker under Moffat. Livingstone started a PR campaign for his friend, writing to the directors in his defence, and asking mutual contacts to drop a good word for him into conversation with the directors.

There was probably an element of self-interest in this, Livingstone seeing his chances of progressing quickly beyond Kuruman in peril, but it brought forth an effusion of praise for Edwards. He was "an excellent friend", of "very great wisdom and prudence", "a most worthy man and more useful among the Bechuanas than any one I know". Since Moffat had left Kuruman to Edwards, he said, "more members have been added to the church than at any former period".

After a few months in Kuruman, Livingstone rode to Bangwaketse. When the devastated Chief Sebeque asked Livingstone why he had conspired to destroy his people and steal all his cattle, Livingstone replied with "a Scotch answer": "Why did you not listen to the advice I sent you last year from the Bakwain country and thus destroy yourself?" His brashness, he believed, cleared the air, and friendship was restored, Sebeque getting his five wives to make Livingstone the local beer – a bitter pink brew thick with maize. "I am still a teetotaler," Livingstone assured his old landlady Margaret Sewell. "But I always take a little of their stuff when it is offered in kindness." The next day being Sunday, Livingstone was delighted when Sebeque decreed that "nothing was to be done on that day but praying to God and hearing the words of the foreigner". Livingstone sang them some hymns, such as "Jesus shall reign where'er the sun", which he had translated into Tswana.

Livingstone paid a brief visit to the Bakgatla, and found that Chief Mosealele had returned to them from the desert and was eager for Livingstone and his friends to live with them. Livingstone said he would pass on the message.

He then went on to the divided Bakwena, and this time stayed with the rival chief Sechele. Sechele's father Motswasele had been kgosi of the whole tribe of 650 families, but was killed in 1822 when Sechele was ten, by rebels who divided the tribe between them. Sechele, after nine years of destitute wanderings, regained one half, while the other remained with Bube. Though Sechele at first resented Livingstone's having bestowed his presence on Bube last time, after he treated his only child "he did not know what to do with me for kindness", Livingstone said, and talked of keeping him there by force.

Sechele was to prove himself a very clever man, but he greatly amused Livingstone by asking for medicine to make him a better hunter. Like other chiefs, Sechele listened sympathetically to Livingstone's preaching, but was not at all convinced. He had some hard and astute questions for his guest: "Since it is true that all who die unforgiven are lost forever," demanded Sechele, "why did your nation not come to tell us of it before now? My ancestors are all gone and none of them knew anything of what you tell me. How is this?"

"I thought immediately of the guilt of the church," says Livingstone, "but did not confess." Instead he said Christians had been too busy converting their own countrymen.

While he was with the Bakwena, a group of female refugees arrived. They were Bakwena prisoners of Mzilikazi's warriors who had escaped and travelled for two months across the desert, eating roots and sleeping on high rocks to avoid recapture, and they looked half-starved. The Bakwena seemed to Livingstone to have not the least sympathy for their ordeal; "They were 'women only'", as he put it. However, his own wagon drivers were frightened by the women's stories and refused to go any further with him, so Livingstone left the wagon with them and continued on ox-back, accompanied by three Bakwena that Sechele sent with him. The ox's loose skin made it hard to stay on, and its habit of butting its rider with its long horns was annoying, and yet having no wheels allowed Livingstone to venture into the Kalahari Desert for the first time.

There he found the Bakalihari, the enslaved tribe of whom he had met women and children on his first outing with Edwards. They were perpetually half-starved and constantly hunting to provide the animal skins their Tswana overlords demanded. They lived in the desert, miles from water, so as to see less of their abusers, and far from their own crops in an attempt to keep their food for themselves. They ate roots, desert fruits, caterpillars, locusts and wild honey. The locusts, Livingstone reckoned, were as good as shrimps, though they tasted rather grassy, and he learned to follow the calls of "honey birds" to find hives. But he was glad of his gun to put some more meat on the menu, including rhino and antelope. On one hunting trip, spying game in a tree, he ran with a dog to catch it, only to see a tiger, hidden a few feet away, leap out and make off with the dog. On another he got lost and had to spend a night alone in a tree listening to the noise of lions and hyenas.

He had the wonderful experience of sitting with the Bakalihari round the fire at night and hearing their stories, and contributed his own about Christ. One story challenged Livingstone's impression that the Tswana had no concept of an afterlife. The story went that God sent the chameleon to tell humans that when they die their spirits fly upward and later return, so the devil sent the quicker black lizard to outrun it and tell humans that death is the end, and not to believe any messenger that comes afterwards.

Livingstone and his Bakwena companions visited the Bakaa high on their black rock, and he broke his finger climbing back down to their camp with a Bible in hand. He then broke it again, shooting at a lion that attacked them in the middle of the night. "As I can bear a little pain, it was not really so great a hindrance as you may imagine," he assured the LMS directors. He only stayed two nights there, because after his companion had been taken ill last time the rumour spread that the Bakaa were up to their old tricks and poisoning visitors, and they were so determined to acquit themselves they gave them nothing to eat but watermelon and sweet reeds.

Livingstone was better satisfied staying with the smaller Makalaka, a tribe one day's walk from Bakaa, where, he wrote to his Blantyre friend James MacLehose, "Their boiled beans were so good we awakened during the night again and again to eat them, and I cut the very buttons off my trousers to give them as tokens of my gratitude." They also gave him roast rhinoceros skin, but he found it too tough to swallow more than two mouthfuls.

Livingstone desperately wanted to go further. The locals told him he was just ten days away from Lake Ngami, which had still not been seen by a white person. But he turned back to the Bakwena. In his published memoir he gave the impression that he was too committed to mission to spare the time for mere tourism, but his letters to Margaret Sewell and others were more candid: the journey would entail crossing part of the Kalahari, and his supplies were in his wagon 200 miles away, guarded by men he was not sure he could trust.

Returning to Kuruman in June 1843, Livingstone had just turned thirty and had reason to feel proud. He was disappointed to be such a long way from converting a single African person, but he had made strategic progress. He had proved himself fearless, enduring and resourceful. As well as breaking bones, meeting big cats, getting sunburnt and eating the porridge of poisoners, he had suffered diarrhoea and constipation, and gone a dangerously long time without food, tying a handkerchief around his waist to relieve hunger pangs. He reckoned his ability to go without water amazed the Tswana and matched their own. Hearing his Bakwena guides once say – assuming that he would not understand them – that he wore trousers to hide his skinny frame and "only appears stout because he puts himself into those bags; he will soon knock up", this gave him all the motivation he needed to keep them all at top speed for days. He had now been 500 miles north-west of Kuruman, which he boasted to Sewell was twice as far as Moffat had ever gone.

"Formerly traders went far beyond missionaries," he told her. "Now I am determined if spared to be outdone by no one in carrying the blessed gospel to the regions beyond. I see it stated Mr Moffat intends to go where no white man has yet been. I can tell you he must go a precious long way for that purpose."

And yet, as he returned to Kuruman and reported on his travels to the directors and other correspondents, his letters reveal a miserable man utterly disillusioned with his calling and who had not hit it off with South Africa. The Tswana were the worst people on earth, immoral, ignorant, foolish and adamantly opposed to the gospel. His colleagues were shockingly quarrelsome, and the land itself was so sparsely populated it was hardly worth the manpower. The Tswana language was inadequate for Christian teaching. He disdained to complain of the physical ordeal of African travel, but he must have wondered whether it was worth it.

Livingstone's reports reveal some striking attitudes at this early stage of his experience. He judged the Tswana to be cowardly and yet murderous, shameless, lazy and incorrigibly polygamous. "Everything about them is so degraded and impure... It would be difficult to point to their inferiors in the world." He was disgusted that they wore scars – some as many as forty – to celebrate the people they had killed, including women and children, and yet faced with danger were "the greatest cowards in the world". Women were expected to do all domestic and agricultural labour "while the 'Lords of the Creation' sew karosses, milk the cattle and hunt or sleep."

His frustration with Tswana attitudes to missionaries shows remarkable expectations about the ease with which a people's way of life and understanding of the universe should be transformed. They could not have been keener to receive his visits or have him stay permanently – "You have come to us just like rain," Sekomi said – but it annoyed Livingstone that their motives were purely practical. They should have been welcoming him because of his message, but inexplicably after hearing it for more than a month in some cases, they showed no interest in converting.

He was frustrated by the Tswana language and its failure to provide words to translate key concepts of Judeo-Christian metaphysics. Its simplicity made it easy to learn, but forced missionaries to use terms "as unlike the idea we intend to convey as is the sound of a wagon wheel". They had to talk about steam when they meant "soul", or dried cowpats when they meant "sin", or the word "made use of when a man sees a nice fat ox" when they meant holiness. Even this Livingstone seemed to see as a moral failing of the Tswana: the Spirit was willing to speak to them in their own language, "but the earthly sense in which the natives have always used the words constitutes a great barrier".

And he was frustrated by the centrality of witchcraft to their view of the world. They saw it as the source – and therefore remedy – of all illness and misfortune. He spoke with repugnance of village holy men who by sleight of hand pretended to cure diseases by "suck[ing] out of the bodies of the sick pieces of bones, skins of animals, ashes, goat's dung, etc. etc.", which evil witches had supposedly put there. He believed the people suspected this was fraud but were too frightened by the holy man's witchcraft to expose him. Naturally they thought of Livingstone's own gifts in terms of witchcraft too – a conception he was willing to use when selling them the idea of irrigation – but it annoyed him when they treated his medicine that way. "They are mere children," he protested.

To be fair to Livingstone, such disparagement was quite standard for missionaries in South Africa at the time. Their various published writings describe their hosts as "wretched and disgusting", "extremely lazy", "without natural affection", "without the smallest marks of civilization", "sunk in many instances below the brutes". Moffat said of the San (or Bushmen), "We can scarcely conceive of human beings descending lower in the scale of ignorance and vice." Even Philip, as enlightened a voice as could be heard on the subject, defended the San by saying that while they were "doubtless in a very ignorant and degraded state" they had the capacity to improve.

It is perhaps worth noticing that Livingstone, like other missionaries, never considered African people "primitive". Rather, they believed that God had made early humans well, so the morals and theology of African heathenism were, in Livingstone's words, an advanced case of "the lamentable deterioration of my species". In a sense though this only made the missionaries less sympathetic towards them, "their depravity being subnatural".

Either way, Livingstone's tone in talking about his Tswana hosts, while sometimes suggesting friendship and loving service, often rather suggests a doctor impatient to cure a population of the disease that is their way of life, and exasperated by their stubborn attachment to it.

Returning to European society in Kuruman in June 1843 was no remedy for Livingstone's depression, and brought fresh annoyances. A delivery of clothes donated by well-wishers in Britain arrived, and in disbelief Livingstone found it full of useless trash, most of it filthy and worn out – ball gowns, parasol fabric, Georgian silk buttons, "old dirty shirt collars for people who have no shirts". Even if they had sent clothes missionaries could have used, it would have been cheaper to buy them in the Cape than to send them from England. Moffat had been telling his audiences that every gift was useful, "but he had no idea people would have such India rubber consciences".

Livingstone even took exception to the news that new LMS missionaries, Walter Inglis and William Ashton and their wives, were coming out to join them. Inglis was a good friend from Ongar whom Livingstone had looked forward to working with, but, Livingstone complained to the directors, South Africa was so sparsely populated, and there were so many missionaries here – twelve not including wives – achieving so little, that any new recruits should have been sent to India or China. He sent the directors a census of the tribes he knew, with a veiled accusation that Moffat had exaggerated the population to get more missionaries there.

The news that China had conceded defeat to Britain in the First Opium War, ceded Hong Kong and opened four ports, allowing missionaries into the country, came to Livingstone as one last twist of the knife. He had to accept the inscrutable wisdom of God, but every other consideration told him he was in the wrong place. "I have..." he confessed, "felt again the glowings of heart towards that country which were familiar to my mind when I dedicated myself to the mission work there. I feel it is wrong to think more of another field than that to which in the providence of God I have been called, and endeavour to suppress my feelings."

Chapter 6

CONFLICT IN MABOTSA

In 1843, the Moffats arrived back in South Africa, and sent ahead a letter they had brought from the LMS directors to Edwards: the directors had agreed to the plan for Edwards and Livingstone to settle with the Bakgatla, as soon as the Moffats were back in Kuruman. With his typical attitude to the letter of his instructions, Livingstone argued that now was the season for building, and if they waited for Moffat they would either be constructing houses in unbearable heat or be delaying the move for another year. Edwards was persuaded – or as Livingstone put it, "I concluded that it would be proper to proceed immediately... [Edwards] resolved to accompany me." So the Edwardses, Livingstone and the Tswana preacher Mebalwe set up their new riverside settlement with the Bakgatla in August 1843, naming it after the neighbouring hill, Mabotsa. They bought three square miles of land from Chief Mosealele for the price of a musket plus ammunition and beads, altogether worth about £4. The Bakgatla were moving as well, getting fresh pasture for their cattle. Livingstone, Edwards and Mebalwe set to work building houses, including a fifty-foot meeting house, and irrigating their land.

The newcomers preached regularly, and their audience listened respectfully, but Livingstone was frustrated to find they could awaken no spiritual curiosity in them. He asked why they had no questions when he had come so far to tell them about God. They replied, "Do we know to ask?" Mosealele started to eat with a knife and fork, but it was small consolation. Their outpost was visited by big game hunters, including Captain Thomas Steele, who remained friends with Livingstone and gave him such invaluable navigational equipment that Livingstone named one of his children after him.

In October, they heard that the Moffat family was travelling up from Cape Town – with, rumour added, fifty tonnes of luggage and big heads from their celebrity in Britain. Livingstone and Edwards went to meet them near the Vaal River, a week's ride south of Kuruman. Livingstone says that he was seized with such thrill at seeing them in the distance his horse ran across the hot plain as if "at Ascot or the Derby". During the week's journey back to Kuruman, Livingstone found Moffat a humble man who understood the Tswana and was more open to the idea of African missionaries than he had supposed. Livingstone's disillusionment with Moffat was swept away.

Livingstone was also reunited with his Ongar friend Walter Inglis, who came as a missionary with the Moffats. Livingstone, in his early months in South Africa, had dreamed of Inglis accompanying him in his pioneering mission, but now his disapproval of new missionaries to Africa made his welcome rather cooler.

Livingstone also met the Moffats' daughter, Mary, for the first time. It would go beyond the evidence to say that he fell in anything so impractical as love, but four years in Africa had worn down his commitment to remaining single and he decided that Mary was the person to deliver him from it. Being an unmarried white man in Kuruman had proved lonely, and for all his independence he felt unlooked-after compared to his male colleagues. His letters home were filled with complaints: "What are you all doing? is a question that I sometimes ask myself, but no answer but the still deathlike quietness which you can almost hear in this wide wilderness land."

Mary was twenty-five and had lived all her life in South Africa. She was as fluent in Tswana as in English and worked at Kuruman in the twin roles expected of missionary wives: teacher and household manager, making clothes, candles and soap. She was not beautiful, but her hardiness, piety and good nature seemed more useful attractions to Livingstone. He described her as, "A matter-of-fact lady, a little, thick, black-haired girl, sturdy, and all that I want." As for what the match offered Mary, her mother was a domineering woman, and the number of other single white men she was likely to meet in South Africa was small, so David offered an opportunity to switch from missionary daughter to missionary wife that might not be repeated.

Returning to Mabotsa, after two weeks in Kuruman, Livingstone decided to propose on his next visit, but the engagement was delayed by a lion. The Bakgatla had been suffering more than ever from lions since their move – they had grown bold enough to attack cattle pens in daylight, from which the Bakgatla concluded they were dealing with witchcraft, making it more dangerous than ever to intervene. On 16 February 1844, lions attacked some villagers' sheep on the other side of the valley, and they called Livingstone and Mebalwe to help. Livingstone wanted to encourage them to kill a lion, as this would disperse the whole pride. Arriving on the scene, they saw the lion thirty yards away on a rock, and Livingstone shot it with both barrels. The villagers ran towards the wounded animal as he started to reload, but hearing a shout he looked up and saw the lion pounce on him. It sank its teeth into his shoulder, and brought him to the ground. "Growling horribly close to my ear, he shook me as a terrier does a rat." Mebalwe shot and misfired, but the lion left Livingstone and attacked Mebalwe, biting his thigh. A third man threw a spear, again diverting the lion, but just as it was taking him by the shoulder it suddenly fell down dead from Livingstone's original shot.

The lion had broken Livingstone's arm and left eleven gashes like gunshot wounds. The Edwardses nursed him in their home,

Rogers setting the bone on Livingstone's instructions, but the wound became seriously infected and Livingstone starved himself to abate the swelling. He argued with the Edwardses and moved out to a hut where he was tended by Mebalwe's family. His letters make almost no mention of the attack, except to reassure those who had already heard about it.

Somehow, by June, they had recovered well enough for Livingstone and Edwards, in turns, to take Mebalwe to twelve villages of neighbouring tribes, training him as a missionary. This was Livingstone's treasured scheme of native agency in practice, but he was starting to feel as disappointed by that as he was by every other aspect of his mission. Certainly Mebalwe was excellent, but he stood alone and he was not getting results. Moffat allowed Livingstone to appeal to Kuruman Christians to volunteer for the work, but none of them wanted to, being "too wedged and dovetailed amongst their relatives". Having fought so hard for the principle, it was embarrassing to have to report to the LMS that it was getting nowhere; and having promoted it endlessly among his correspondents, it was humiliating to receive a donation of £15 from a Southampton Sunday school to pay for another African teacher, and have to donate it to the LMS general fund because he had no one to give it to. "We have fine scenery," Livingstone said, "the vegetation luxuriant... abundance of excellent water" but spiritually it was "a vast howling wilderness".

Livingstone went to Kuruman in July 1844 and a little nervously proposed to Mary as they sat under a fruit tree. She distrusted him at first, but soon accepted him, and when he returned to Mabotsa in August it was to build a family home with the help of a villager from Kuruman. It had stone walls to a height of four foot, topped with mud. It was meant to be all stone, until Livingstone badly hurt his recovering left arm when he instinctively caught a falling stone with his left hand, and the jolt nearly broke it again. "It is pretty hard work," he wrote to his fiancée, apologizing for soiling the paper with his muddy hands, "and almost enough to drive love out of my head, but it is not situated there; it is in my heart, and won't come out unless you behave so as to quench it!"

Edwards completed the school and Mebalwe and Livingstone taught in it, reluctantly in the latter case. The children were also tearful and afraid, having heard that white men bit children and fed them with human brains, but both parties got used to it. Mebalwe taught them the alphabet to the tune of "Auld Lang Syne". Livingstone was irritated to find attendance fluctuating between fifty and two, and church attendance was equally erratic, depending on the influence of Chief Mosealele. However high attendance was, no one showed any interest in what was taught there. "Their mind is darkness itself," said Livingstone.

Lush though their valley was, they suffered a dry year. Drought brought a rainmaker to Mabotsa, a small man with wrinkly eyes and plaited hair, and Livingstone took him on. He privately told the rainmaker his powers were an iniquitous swindle, and the rainmaker responded by publicly blaming him for the drought. When Livingstone challenged the Bakgatla to test the rainmaker, he was told, "White men know how to make guns, and black men know how to make rain, and the latter ought not to be interfered with." Livingstone persuaded him to announce when the rain would come, repeatedly proving him wrong. Livingstone also got a laugh by pointing out that the smoke the man sent up to heal the clouds was going in the wrong direction. And yet none of this made any impact on the Bakgatlas' faith in and fear of the rainmaker's powers. Rather, as the drought continued, their suspicion grew that the anti-rainmaking missionaries did not want them to have rain.

By the end of 1844, Livingstone's house was finished, with the stately dimensions of fifty-two by twenty feet. "The greater heat of the climate", he explained to the directors, "required greater dimensions than at stations farther south." He headed to Kuruman for the wedding, confiding in a letter home that he had been happy single and "cannot leave the bachelor life without a sigh". While in town, he made proposals for a seminary to train African evangelists. This got no support from anyone: the other missionaries felt African Christians were too few and too spiritually immature to make it work. Livingstone was pained to hear another nail being hammered into the coffin of his treasured policy, and argued with them, making unflattering comparisons between their own achievements and those to be expected from black preachers, and accusing them of overmanning Kuruman when they should be venturing north. As a result of this argument, his old friend Inglis entered the list of his enemies.

David and Mary were married on 2 January 1845, and then he brought her back to her new home. It seemed to David time for a new start at Mabotsa. Their services so far had not achieved anything he had hoped for, he reflected, so he planned a series of scientific lectures, starting with the subject of iron. The idea was to challenge their magical understanding of it, show them how to make better practical use of it, and give them better reason to accept the notion of a benevolent creator. And on the principle of a bird in the hand, he would spend more time teaching the children in Mebalwe's family. And yet his eyes were still on the far horizon: he wrote to a friend, "I don't expect to remain there long. The sphere is too small for two missionaries."

The move came sooner than expected. He and Mary arrived at Mabotsa to an emotional storm that ensured it would not be their home for long. To David's astonishment, Edwards was furious with him, and they fell out violently.

Livingstone took notes on their argument, and wrote about it at inordinate length, mostly in private letters to Moffat but also in a long official account to the LMS directors. And yet it is still not entirely clear what happened. We only have Livingstone's account of their falling out, and he is a one-sided witness at the best of times, of which this was not one. What follows is a cautious reconstruction.

The trigger seems to have been a letter which Livingstone had written to the LMS directors describing the establishment of Mabotsa, and which was published in the *Missionary Magazine and Chronicle* in April 1844. The editor's extract included no mention of Edwards by name, leaving Livingstone talking merely about "we". The introduction to the report said, "Our intrepid Missionary, Mr Livingston…, has made preparatory arrangements for the opening of a station among the tribe of Bakhatla."

Edwards read the magazine and felt that Livingstone was blatantly undermining him. This brought two incidents back to mind: one six months earlier when he felt Livingstone had undermined his discipline of a local woman over a trivial incident involving food; the other from fourteen months before when, conversely, a man involved in an altercation with Livingstone had appealed to Edwards, and Livingstone insisted on settling the matter himself. Then there was the fact that Livingstone had been monopolizing Mebalwe, treating the only Tswana teacher in Mabotsa as his personal employee.

Their relative authority was a sensitive issue for Edwards. He had long been subservient to Moffat, lacked confidence in his role in the LMS, and as a layman had faced opposition to his establishment of Mabotsa. And now he had finally founded his own mission station it seemed that Livingstone was trying to take it over, "to drive things all [his] own way" and make Edwards a "mere appendix". This fear was fed when he and his wife exchanged letters with the Rosses at Kuruman, who considered Livingstone ambitious and manipulative among other faults.

So, as soon as David and Mary arrived in January 1845, Edwards accused him of being "dishonest, dishonourable, and mischievous". Livingstone asked for particulars, Edwards reminded him of the two distant incidents, saying, according to Livingstone's account, "You went to the natives, Sir, you went to the natives, and there is not a better way of destroying their confidence in my integrity than this."

They argued about this at length, but it became clear to Livingstone that the heart of the problem, "the root of bitterness from which most of the other evils have sprung", was the *Chronicle* article and his supposed ambitions for Mabotsa. Livingstone could have put Edwards's mind at rest by explaining the editorial mishap, and saying that his ambition was not to take over Mabotsa but to go further into the interior. Instead, astonishingly, Livingstone replied that Edwards did not deserve the credit for founding Mabotsa anyway, because he, Livingstone, had done it himself. Edwards, he said, had originally had in mind a different site thirty miles away, while Livingstone had always favoured this one, and it was Livingstone who got Chief Mosealele's approval on a solo visit, while Edwards "merely slowed them down" by dithering about the directors' approval.

Edwards showed Livingstone a long letter he had written to the directors complaining about him. In it Edwards insisted he was "not the mere appendix Mr Livingstone wishes him to be", informed them of Livingstone's wanting to start building without waiting for permission from London, and complained of "Mr Livingstone's well-known sentiments... that native teachers are superior to English labourers." Edwards later amended the letter, and then never sent it.

Instead Mr and Mrs Edwards left Mabotsa in April for Motito, 200 miles away, to appeal against Livingstone to the new international missionary committee.

In Livingstone's defence, there were probably failings on both sides in this unedifying squabble, Edwards perhaps being oversensitive and letting old resentments fester. There was perhaps a political dimension, Edwards and others resenting Moffat's dominance, and fearing that David's marriage to Mary would act as an alliance. Livingstone certainly had no desire to take over Mabotsa, and the offence of the *Chronicle* article was not his fault.

And yet paradoxically the article is a pretty fair example of what was offensive in his attitude to Edwards. Livingstone's excessive autonomy made him think and talk about mission almost entirely in terms of what *he* was doing towards *his* goals, to the extent that all his letters about reconnoitring for and founding Mabotsa described it as if it were his own personal project. Writing about Mabotsa to Mrs Sewell, he said, "I deeply regret taking Mr Edwards there," and when he wrote his missionary autobiography in 1857, the section on Mabotsa did not mention the existence of Edwards once. It was obviously extremely important to Edwards to found a new station, jointly manage it and have this work recognized – reasonable expectations that Livingstone failed to allow. Livingstone could have made peace by reassuring Edwards and giving him public acknowledgment. He did the opposite, consolidating their enmity by promoting in his letters and published writing an absurdly pedantic and mean-spirited version of events in which Edwards played no part in his founding of Mabotsa. As soon as the breach between them happened, Livingstone was unable to see Edwards as anything but an enemy.

Even after the Edwardses left, the quarrel ground on in Livingstone's mind, and he found himself obsessing over his grievances when he should have had his mind on higher things. He picked over earlier events and reinterpreted them, deciding that Mrs Ross had turned the Edwardses against him from the start, and that Mr Edwards had been conspiring to get Livingstone out of Mabotsa. In the words of John Kirk, a later colleague and friend who learned the knack of staying in his good books, "Dr L, if he once takes an ill opinion of anyone, makes up into a devil very soon, by working together all imaginable things... He is a man who takes small intense hatreds and is therefore a more dangerous enemy than useful friend."

Livingstone wrote constantly to Moffat, supposedly with news, but filling his letters with all the complaints and retorts to the Rosses, Edwardses and Inglis that he never had made to their faces. He congratulated himself on his restraint for not talking to them frankly about their "most abominable muleheaded wickedness". Throughout his career, Livingstone's relationships were blighted by the fact that he made a virtue out of non-communication, advising his son, "Seldom show that you are displeased."

Livingstone had plenty of time to reflect on the progress of his work. He had been two years in Mabotsa, and achieved nothing but building and bickering. The Bakgatla cared nothing for his meetings, even his new science lectures, and they blamed the Europeans for the drought they were suffering. They had not taken a step nearer Christianity and could not be expected to as long as Livingstone and Edwards were fighting there. It was time to move on.

Two hundred miles away in Motito, Edwards heard what Livingstone had never told him, that he had ambitions beyond Mabotsa. Returning briefly in August 1845 en route to the Cape Colony, he told Livingstone, "I cannot but regret that I was not previously aware of your wish. Had I been, I might have waived all matters of difference between us." The breach was too great to be mended now though. LMS rules naturally required the Livingstones to stay with the Bakgatla until Mr and Mrs Edwards returned permanently, but his heart had moved already and he decided that he and Mary would quit Mabotsa in their absence, and start a new mission station with another tribe. Chief Mosealele was offended to find that they were leaving, and asked, Livingstone said, if they were "tired because the hearts of the Bakhatla were hard. He [Mosealele] explained that the hearts of all the Bechuanas were so and he could observe that they were just about to begin to give way to the preaching of the word." Livingstone did not believe him, but could not help having a bad conscience as he planned his escape.

Chapter 7

DROUGHT IN CHONWANE

The Bakwena were the obvious choice for Livingstone's next mission field, and he convinced himself that they were "less degraded" than the Bakgatla. But they were divided between the two chiefs and Livingstone wavered between them. Bube assured him, unconvincingly, that he was terribly keen on the word of God, while Sechele gave him more plausible reasons for wanting him: medicine, gun mending, protection, and reading lessons. The last point impressed Livingstone – Sechele seemed to have more interest in "civilization" than other kgosi – and Sechele clinched the deal with one of his awkward questions: "When we reach the presence of God, will you be able to say you have taught us? I shall tell him you have not."

When Livingstone demanded to know what Sechele thought he had done when he visited them before if not teaching, Sechele replied, "But can we know by being told once?"

So David, the pregnant Mary, and Mebalwe and his family quit Mabotsa, and settled forty miles away in Chonwane with Sechele's Bakwena. Edwards was annoyed that Livingstone had poached Mebalwe, but Livingstone insisted that Mebalwe was so attached to him he could not bear to stay – which may have been a slight overstatement, but basically true. As a rule, Livingstone's relationships across the cultural divide were as successful as those within his own culture were disastrous.

A new Tswana preacher joined them there, a Kuruman deacon called Paul. Africans were given names from the English Bible when they were baptized, Mebalwe's being David. Livingstone preferred to use their Tswana name, but Paul was an exception because his old name meant "Father of Darkness". Livingstone bought land for the three families with a gun, ammunition and beads, and once again they started building and gardening.

If playing host to a missionary was supposed to bring luck to a kgosi, the immediate results were ambiguous for Sechele. While the arrangements were being made, he gave or sold twelve pounds of gunpowder to Bube. After using some on an unsuccessful elephant hunt, Bube decided it was insufficiently enchanted, so he tried to re-enchant the gunpowder with burning medicine. The explosion killed him. Sechele laid claim to Bube's followers, and a number of leading men came over to him. Bube's successor, Kgakge, kept hold of their possessions and wives and children, expecting Sechele's tribe to fight for them, as per tradition, but Livingstone persuaded Sechele to try diplomacy to avoid violence. Sure enough Kgakge ceded the possessions and people, and further people came with them, but some weeks later some of Sechele's men were assaulted by Kgakge's, and taunted about the cowardice of their tribe. Sechele had to admit that he had tarnished the honour of his people by failing to fight for what was theirs, so, telling Livingstone he was taking them elephant hunting, he armed them and attacked Kgakge's tribe. The latter were decimated and had to take shelter at Mabotsa, finally reuniting with Sechele six years later.

Sechele is described by a number of travellers as tall, dark-skinned, good-looking and charismatic. The hunter Henry Methuen met him clothed in grey catskin, with brass rings on arms and legs and four red feathers in his hair. He took to literacy with alacrity, learning the alphabet, upper and lower case, in two days. He quickly learned to read Tswana words in Roman letters, compiling his own spelling books, and set about reading Moffat's translations of the Bible. He ate breakfast before sunrise in order to start school as quickly as possible, and then taught his five wives to read. They took some persuading because they feared quite rightly that the white people's monogamous faith put them in a precarious position, but they learned well. Other leading Bakwena people followed Sechele's example, but had less leisure time to devote to it and so – Livingstone being unable to provide the reading medicine they wanted – they had much less success.

Mary and David's first child, Robert, was born in January 1846 while the new town was still being built. David explained to his father that he would have followed tradition in naming him Neil "if it were not such an ugly name". He brought trees from Mabotsa, and the door and window frames from their old house, having been disgusted to hear that Inglis would inherit it, and deciding that Edwards would find it easy enough to make new ones. He heard that Mrs Ross had died of dysentery, and said that it was "a great loss to her husband and children, but to no one else". Livingstone slipped while building the roof of his house, and found himself swinging from the arm that he had broken, which put him out of action for a while. Sechele built a wall round town with loopholes for guns.

Drought seemed to have followed them from Mabotsa and the water supply at Chonwane dried up. "The corn is short, burned, and shooting into ear about two feet from the ground," Livingstone told Moffat. For all his derision of Tswana superstition, he could not help asking, "Is it the Prince of the Power of the Air who ranges drought at Chonwane, as was last season at Mabotsa?" The Bakwena had to commute to the well-watered ground of Kolobeng forty miles away and replant their crops there. None of this put Sechele off his studies, though Livingstone seemed to find his interest at least as puzzling as it was gratifying, reporting to Moffat: "Strange to say, he goes on reading and listens to preaching with as much attention as ever."

In February, Livingstone received a letter from the Commandant of the Transvaal Boers wanting to know what he was doing in Chonwane, which was near the western border of Transvaal. The Boers had settled there after routing the Zulu kingdom of Mzilikazi, claiming all his former domains and enslaving the large numbers of Tswana who still lived there. As we have seen, their Great Trek out of British territory was a result of the abolition of slavery there and the extension of equal legal rights to black people, and since the latter was the work of missionaries they were highly suspicious of British missionary expansion as a threat to their freedom to enslave. The Commandant threatened to come and disarm Sechele's Bakwena, and wanted an assurance from Livingstone that he would not preach in or send preachers into Transvaal without their sanction.

Livingstone was extremely reluctant to give such an assurance, especially as he had already received an application for a missionary from Mokhatla, a Tswana chief in Transvaal. So, in July, David, Mary and Paul crossed the Limpopo into Transvaal to talk with the Boers and spy out the land, with the hope that Paul would stay and preach. Being hungry, weak and ill they also hoped to return healthier and better fed.

They found Transvaal far more densely populated with Tswana than anywhere else they had been, and rich in ore and cattle. Having on previous journeys gone for more than a week without seeing anyone, they met people every day. They met a kgosi who made copper wire. They met a tribe who produced artefacts from a tin–copper amalgam, whose kgosi at twenty years of age had forty-eight wives and twenty children, and said that the Boers had recently raided his tribe and taken thirty cattle and fifty sheep. Another kgosi showed them stripes on his back inflicted by Boers. They heard how the Boers forced three tribes to form their front line when they raided a fourth tribe to seize 10,000 sheep and 400 people. Everywhere he heard that kgosi were forced to supply children as slaves on a twenty-year term. "When we came," Livingstone said, "the people ran up the rocks in fear and the chief told me the reason was the Boers came into their towns, drunk their beer and abused their women." "I was quite ashamed to be called a Sekoa," he added, *Sekoa* being the Tswana word for European.

Livingstone met the Commandant, supplied medicine to the Boers and gained permission to continue his mission. But he did not overcome their essential hostility. One Boer told him he might as well teach baboons as Africans. Livingstone challenged him to a reading and writing competition with "one of these baboons" – Paul – but he declined. When Mokhatla, the chief who had applied for a missionary, told Livingstone that he had more than once been told by a Boer neighbour to kill Livingstone, he decided it was not safe to leave Paul there. Once more his passion for native agency was thwarted, and he was humiliated to return home to Chonwane to find a letter from the LMS reminding him how vital it was. Moffat, who opposed native agency, pointed out to the directors that Livingstone alone among missionaries had had two African teachers, "the two best", and had achieved nothing with them at all.

Baby Robert had been very ill on the journey, and their supplies ran out on the way home. Faced with having to get Robert across the Limpopo in flood again, Mary burst into tears. "The journey did me good," Livingstone reckoned, "but my better half became as thin as a lath." They arrived at Chonwane to hear that the second crop planted by the Bakwena at Kolobeng had been eaten by buffaloes. Mary and Robert retreated to Kuruman to recover.

The settlement in Chonwane was not proving a success. The missionaries' preaching was not popular. "To be plain with you," one villager told Livingstone, "we should like you much better if you traded with us and then went away, without forever boring us with preaching that 'word of God' of yours." Others insisted they loved having them there – except for the preaching. The drought dragged on and the villagers concluded it was caused by the Livingstones' house, so he allowed them to sprinkle the roof with medicine to cure it, to no avail.

Livingstone and Sechele agreed they were going to have to move permanently to Kolobeng, the better watered site where their crops were planted. This would be a further embarrassment for Livingstone, it would mean giving up his hope of settling Paul in Transvaal, and it would be financially disastrous. Livingstone was already £29 in debt for the building materials for his houses in Mabotsa and Chonwane, and he had made too many enemies to beg £20 from the local committee for a third. Household goods were expensive enough in the Cape Colony, but their price doubled and more by the time they reached Chonwane. The Rosses and Edwardses took long leaves to go south and stock up, which provoked Livingstone's derision: "If you meet me down in the colony before eight years are expired you may shoot me." So his only recourse was to write asking the LMS directors for help – though they had recently announced that their funds were low and they were cutting funding for South Africa, a policy that Livingstone could hardly dispute after his complaints about overstaffing there.

Continued drought meant work for the rainmaker, and among the Bakwena Sechele took those duties upon himself. Though Livingstone tried to persuade him that it was pointless folly, he had no better alternative to offer. The Bakwenas reiterated that, just as God had given medicine to Europeans, he had given rainmaking to Africans. Livingstone asked why, in that case, it did not seem to work. He was told, "Your medicines produce no visible effect either when you administer them, but they enter into the inward parts, do their work and then the cure follows many days afterwards. In like manner our rain medicines enter into the clouds, heal them, and we have rain sometime afterwards."

Sechele gave him a fascinating insight into his attitude to witchcraft after a European trader visited Chonwane and sold the chief a pinch of hugely overpriced sulphur as medicine to help him shoot better. Sechele happily inserted it under the skin of his trigger hand, and of course Livingstone insisted it was pointless. To prove Sechele had been duped into believing this was a valuable potion, he gave him a whole cupful of the stuff. Sechele stared at it sadly and said, "I wish you would deceive me too."

Sechele was by far the most promising cloud in Livingstone's barren sky. His literacy and divinity are hard to disentangle as the only reading he had was the Bible, but he loved it. By 1847 he could read it himself, and it captured his imagination in a way Livingstone's preaching never had. He discussed it with Livingstone constantly, and as a result forbade his people to garden or hunt on Sundays. Mary taught around sixty children every afternoon.

The way of the Bible seemed to bring with it a taste for European culture, as Sechele ordered a mattress, lanterns, candles, an iron, a table and soap from Kuruman, and adopted European clothing, including a red coat, shirt, cap, and handkerchief, and a suit made from hartebeest skin. The coat he kept for Sundays. Livingstone was unwilling to read too much into Sechele's Europhile tastes: "Unless they are converted," he said, "advance in civilization will be a poor reward for our toils."

Even as the unprecedented drought continued into 1847, Sechele renounced rainmaking – though he allowed his people to send for a rival rainmaker. The only barrier left between Sechele and Livingstone's Christ was the formidable one of the kgosi's five wives. This was not simply a matter of an individual's way of life: conversion would mean sending four women home as ex-wives, two of them to other tribes, and as in European dynasties marriage created political union between leading families, so divorcing the daughters of his elders would threaten the unity of the Bakwena. An added twist was that three of Sechele's wives were becoming excellent Bible students, while his principal wife, Selemeng, was hostile to the gospel.

Livingstone had become aware of the problems of dismantling African traditions of polygamy while preaching to the Bakgatla in Mabotsa. In an intriguing exchange of letters with John Parker, an Ongar friend who was now in Calcutta, he had put the case for toleration: the Bible says the only valid ground for divorce is adultery, so polygamy is not sufficient cause; the New Testament explicitly forbids polygamy, but as the Old Testament

allows it this cannot be the universal law of God; when Hagar
escaped from a polygamous relationship with Abraham, God
commanded her to return; and "I am not aware that Christianity
gives any licence for assaulting the civil institutions of man." But
he concluded that as he was not certain either way, he would
follow the tradition of other missionaries.

So when Sechele asked Livingstone if God would accept a
compromise and receive him if he "acted justly, fairly avoided
fighting, treated both his own people and strangers kindly,
killed witches and prayed to God", quite apart from his horror
at the execution of suspected witches, Livingstone insisted that
monogamy was non-negotiable. As he told the LMS when he
was first living with Sechele, "He says he wishes we had come
to his country before he married so many."

In mid-1847, with Mary heavily pregnant, Livingstone had
to swallow at least some of his pride and take the family to
Kuruman to buy food.

> *I can bear what other Europeans would consider*
> *hunger and thirst without any inconvenience, but*
> *when we arrived to hear the old women who had seen*
> *my wife depart about two years before, exclaiming at*
> *the door, "Bless me! How lean she is! Has he starved*
> *her? Is there no food in the country to which he has*
> *been?" etc. this was more than I could well bear.* [7]

They stayed at Kuruman until their second child was born,
naming her after David's mother, despite his considering
Agnes almost as ugly a name as Neil. As soon as they returned
to Chonwane, they gave up on its parched soils, packed and
moved to Kolobeng, crossing what is now the South African
border into Botswana.

Chapter 8

SALVATION IN KOLOBENG

Coming to Kolobeng, Sechele announced that he would have a magnificent church built at his own expense: "It shall be my work to build a house for God who is the defence of my town." While Livingstone welcomed his enthusiasm (though he found Sechele's hope of winning God's approval through good deeds theologically suspect), he insisted that the building should be a quick temporary one of poles and reeds so they could get down to the urgent business of farming. He also insisted that the Christians share the labour: "It is for the God of all so we shall all work at it." They began on Saturday, met in it on Sunday, and finished it on Tuesday.

They built temporary huts for themselves for the same reason, and though the work was quick, it was hard, this being the hot season, with "all burning Africa spread out before us", and Mary suffered shooting pains in her chest. But at last they had water. David lay awake at night, thrilled to hear the gurgling of the Kolobeng River and the whistling of its frogs – a more beautiful sound, he thought, than all the nightingales, thrushes, blackbirds and canaries in Britain.

While the building continued, Sechele lived in a tent with greased walls and a floor of dried grass, so when he left a candle burning there after a beery evening with his men, it was no great surprise that the whole thing went up in flames. It was perhaps more remarkable that the 100 lb of gunpowder he kept there survived. "All agreed it was a great deliverance," Livingstone said.

The Euro-friendly chief struck a deal with Livingstone: he
and his men would dig the watercourse and build the dam for
him in return for a European-style house – square, with doors
and windows – once their crops were planted. He had taken
to praying, walking through the fields and the huts, and in
September 1847, Sechele asked Livingstone to lead a regular
prayer meeting in his house for himself and his dependants.
"He added," Livingstone says, "he knew he was living in sin
but, though he had not given up those with whom he sinned,
he wished to pray in his family and hoped that some of his
people would be brought to believe." He impressed Livingstone
by leading prayers himself, beautifully. Sometimes when the
missionaries preached, Livingstone saw Sechele's eyes glisten
and knew the gospel was getting through.

Early in 1848, Sechele made a last-ditch attempt to accept Christ
without the shame and cruelty of sending his wives home. He
proposed leaving the Bakwena for a few years' theological study,
assuming that by the time he returned the women would have
found new husbands. Nothing came of that desperate idea, and
on 7 August Sechele announced that he was becoming a Christian
and divorcing, as Livingstone put it, "his superfluous wives".

Sechele's people responded with an outrage that shocked
him – he told Livingstone that in the past he would have shot
anyone who cursed him like this. Instead he told them that if
they wanted to kill him they should do it straightaway. The
women, who did all the farming, went on strike, and there were
night-time meetings about the crisis. Incredibly, drought had
followed them from Chonwane to Kolobeng. The pitiless skies
withheld the rain, the river shrank, and the Bakwena suffered
a third year of scarcity. They had never known anything like
this. It would have been astonishing if they had not blamed
Livingstone and his word of God.

Of the two wives who had come from other tribes, one,
Mokgokong, was allowed to stay with the Bakwenas as she
had no family left to go to, but the other, Makhari, was sent

away, leaving her children. In tears, she returned her Bible to Livingstone, saying that "there is no word of God" where she was going. On her way home, Chief Mosealele of the Bakgatla met her and tried to make Sechele's loss his gain; when Makhari refused to go with him he forbade churchgoing in Mabotsa.

Another Tswana kgosi, Moshesh, sent Sechele a message: "Tell him to allow his people to believe if they like, but he must never believe. I am a king and I won't put myself under the authority of another. I have my kingdom as well as he and people would laugh at me if I believed and put myself under the authority of another. Tell Sechele that."

Sechele being his first success in seven years in South Africa, erring on the side of credulity would have been understandable for Livingstone, but he did the opposite. Despite the evidence of his growing commitment to Christianity over three years, the sacrifices he had made for it and the opposition he had suffered, when Sechele asked for baptism Livingstone gave him a two-month trial period. "I feel my heart trembling", he told Moffat, "when I think of the danger of receiving one who may not be a true believer or refusing one who is."

In the meantime, the Bakwena suffered their hottest and hungriest year ever. Kolobeng had enjoyed just one good shower in 1848, and the river shrank so much that hyenas gathered to collect dead fish. Livingstone measured temperatures of 133°F with his thermometer three inches underground. By November the canal had dried completely, and yet they could watch rain falling in the hills ten miles away. Their crops failed for a fourth time and fruit trees died. The Bakwena, Livingstone reports, complained to Sechele, saying, "'There is Mosealele, he has plenty of rain and he hates the word. Our chief loves it and we have none.' This is the fourth year of scarcity. They had always had abundance of rain until the word came."

Sechele was baptized on 1 October 1848. British supporters of the LMS sent a present of two chairs for him and his wife, which caused great excitement and arrived just in time for the service.

The tribe watched the ceremony in tears of misery; not least because they had heard that baptism involved drinking human brains and that the Eucharist was a kind of orgy – uncannily like the rumours about early Christians in the Roman Empire. One old man said to Livingstone, "You might have delayed till we got rain."

In December, Livingstone and Paul took another journey into Transvaal, to try again to place him as a teacher with Chief Mokhatla. When the Boer Commandant heard what Livingstone was doing, he accused him of spying and arming the Tswana for an attack, and he threatened to send troops against Mokhatla. Livingstone insisted he had no connection with any government and would continue his work "by the authority of Christ". The Commandant offered to tolerate the mission, Livingstone reported, "if I should 'promise to teach the natives that the Boers are a superior race to them'!" He declined the proposal, but met the Commandant along with church officials. The Commandant said he would support Livingstone if he postponed placing Paul for a month while he won round his opponents. So he and Paul returned to Kolobeng in January 1849, only to hear that the Commandant had written to the missionary committee in the meantime demanding Livingstone be removed.

Mary Livingstone gave birth to a third child, Thomas Steele, in March 1849, and then, worn out by life and work in Kolobeng, took the children to Kuruman.

Around the same time, Livingstone made two devastating discoveries. The first was that Paul's son Isak had got a woman pregnant, which Livingstone discovered when she died in childbirth. Paul and Mebalwe, among many others, had known but not told him about it, which left Livingstone feeling betrayed and mocked. He disciplined Mebalwe, but forgave him. He told Paul to leave Kolobeng, but he refused to go.

The second revelation was that Sechele's ex-wife Mokgokong was also pregnant. Livingstone confronted Sechele, who confessed that he had fallen. Livingstone was shattered and told him, "My heart is broken. First Isak, then you. I can no longer be a teacher here."

Sechele replied, "Do not give me up because of this. I shall never give up Jesus. You and I will stand before him together." Livingstone suspended Sechele from communion as Congregational Church rules required, and assumed this would be the end of their friendship. David and Mary agreed that it was time to go north and find another tribe to try the gospel on. And yet Sechele accepted his discipline humbly and amicably, showing no inclination to give up on his relationship with the missionaries or their God. So Livingstone decided – almost reluctantly, it seems – that it was not all over in Kolobeng, and agreed to readmit Sechele sometime after his baby was born.

The idea of going north, however, once Livingstone had tried it on, was not so easy to put aside. He had been with the Bakwena for four years, felt that his "mountain in labour brought forth a ridiculous mouse", and was once again restless. Whatever Livingstone's strengths as a missionary, the humble patience required to attach oneself to one community and stay year after year, preaching the word and leaving the results in God's hands, was not among them.

The thought of the north gripped him all the more thanks to two coincidences. One was that he was visited by a delegation from Chief Lechulatebe of the Batawana tribe who lived near Lake Ngami, which Livingstone had dreamed of "discovering", and they asked for a missionary to live with them. The other was that he heard from the big game hunter William Cotton Oswell who had once passed through Mabotsa when Livingstone was there and had kept in touch ever since. He and his team were on their way up from the Cape on a fabulously well-equipped expedition to the fabled lake, and planned to visit Kolobeng en route. This would be Livingstone's best chance to reach Ngami, and his last to claim its discovery.

Thanks to Sechele's Christian perseverance, Livingstone could not simply abandon the Bakwena, but, as he explained it to Moffat, with the building work at Kolobeng complete and whatever time the townspeople might have had for school or church taken up with foraging to survive the drought, there was frustratingly little for him to do: "I begin to think if another station were in existence on which to spend a part of the year it might tend to the furtherance of the gospel."

It sounds more like an excuse for restlessness than a genuine mission strategy. The truth is that Livingstone's heart was no longer in evangelism – not in doing it himself, that is. By his own evaluation, he had not yet been successful as a missionary, his seed falling on stony ground, and he told himself he needed to find better soil; it seems more accurate to say he was an unsuccessful missionary precisely because he was incapable of staying in one place long enough. Whichever way one looks at it, his evangelistic career had not proved a success, and the fact is that it was now more or less over. He was now looking – however unfocused the search may have been in his own mind – for something else. Pure exploration was more alluring, but would be hard to justify to Livingstone's Christian conscience; it had to be at the service of a greater good. And anyway, who would employ him as an explorer?

These questions remained unanswered, and only half-asked, as Livingstone set off on his Ngami expedition. But Livingstone's evangelistic career had borne all the fruit it would ever bear. Before they left Kolobeng, Livingstone received a letter from the LMS, acknowledging somewhat testily his move there from Chonwane, asking once again what progress he had made in settling a Tswana evangelist with another tribe, and saying, "We hope we may now regard you as permanently settled." Their hope was seriously ill-founded.

Chapter 9

LAKE NGAMI

William Cotton Oswell was an unlikely friend for a man like Livingstone. Educated at Rugby School in Thomas Arnold's day, and at East India College, Haileybury, a highflier who loved sport and literature, he had been given a post in Madras because his uncle was a director of the East India Company and became famous while there as an elephant catcher. He first went to Africa to recover from fever in 1844, spent two years hunting, and stayed briefly with the Livingstones, finding David "the best, most modest and most intelligent of the missionaries" and leaving a wagon as a gift. The only thing they seemed to have in common was that they were linguists, but they became very good friends.

Oswell arrived in Kolobeng with a fellow hunter, Mungo Murray, on an expedition to Ngami equipped with twenty horses, eighty oxen, two wagons, a dozen drivers, and supplies including 300 lb of coffee and 150 lb of shot. Sechele added thirty of his own men to the party, to bring back ivory for him – their Batawana visitors told them tusks were so large and abundant there they made cattle pens out of them – and the British trader J. H. Wilson joined them for the same spoils.

They left Kolobeng on 1 June 1849. At first their main problem was forestry, and they cut down hundreds of trees to make way for the wagons. Then their route crossed the edge of the Kalahari Desert. Livingstone had planned to visit the Bamangwato and Bakalahari, whom he had not met with for seven years, but he saw little of either. Chief Sekomi of the Bamangwato was an ivory trader and feared that Europeans finding their own way to Ngami would be bad for business, so he refused to meet the explorers and tried to drive the Bakalahari away to stop them helping them.

Progress was painfully slow as the oxen dragged wagons through the deep soft sand, and more than once the explorers went for three days without water. They dug eight-foot wells – which Sekomi then filled – fell foul of mirages, and at one point some of the drivers had to take the oxen back twenty miles for water to prevent them dying of thirst.

Five weeks and 300 miles from Kolobeng, they came upon the River Zouga (now called the Botletle). There they met the Bayeiye, a people unrelated to the Tswana – by whom they were considered slaves – darker skinned and with a different language. They navigated the river in canoes made from hollowed-out tree trunks, fished with nets and harpooned hippos. Livingstone preached to them and believed they understood him better on a first hearing than any previous audience. Listening to their stories, he found that they had a name for God, and he thought he heard something similar to Adam and Eve, and the flood. Perhaps northern tribes had fallen less far from the truth and would be less resistant to Christianity?

They followed the river, lined with palms and giant baobab trees, for 280 miles, and finally reached the lake that had been Livingstone's goal for as long as he had been in Africa, but by the time they got there he had all but lost interest in it. The reason was that, before it reached Lake Ngami, the river was joined by another from the north, the Tamunakle. The water at the junction seemed so cold and soft that Livingstone thought it must come from melting snow. The locals told him it was connected to other rivers and they were all navigable. "They seem to me to form a highway into a large section of country," Livingstone wrote to Moffat. "The prospect of this being opened up for missionaries makes the discovery of the Lake dwindle into nothing." He had found a way into the heart of Africa, and evidence that it was not the scorched desert everyone assumed.

What was more, he heard that the Tamunakle would take him to the Makololo, a huge and powerful group ruled by the great warrior chief Sebitwane, whose capital, Linyanti, had a population of 6,000. Livingstone pictured hospitable temperate highlands, densely populated, and connected to the east or west coast by navigable rivers, so that though 1,200 miles from Cape Town (as the crow flies) it would be easier for missionaries to get to than Kuruman. "If spared to effect this", he told Mrs Sewell, "we should then probably be allowed to introduce the gospel into a large and populous region of at least equal importance to the entire Bechuana mission." Livingstone had found a way to make an important contribution to Christian mission, to which he was so passionately committed, which did not depend on his own evangelistic abilities and stickability – opening new territory for other missionaries.

The travellers took a look at the lake and collected their ivory, repeatedly falling into the disguised holes dug by the Bayeiye to catch game. Oswell wanted to bring back some native skulls for a relative, but found Africans too "touchy" about them. Livingstone then wanted to press on north up the Tamunakle. Oswell agreed, but the Batawana did not. They wanted a missionary to stay with them, not go up the river to the Makololo, their powerful enemies, and sell them guns. Oswell had brought no boat so they could not cross the Zouga without the help of the Bayeiye, whom the Batawana kept by force on the opposite bank. Livingstone built rafts, but one kind of wood was too heavy, another too worm-eaten. "I could easily have swam across, and fain would have done it, but landing stark naked and bullying the Bakoba [i.e. Bayeiye] for the loan of a boat would scarcely be the thing for a messenger of peace, even though no alligator met me in the passage."

Oswell saved Livingstone's dream of forging a river path into the interior, by offering to go to the Cape and bring back a boat. Oswell himself dreamed of finding a way to the Zambezi, thereby connecting the Cape Colony with Portuguese trading stations on the east coast.

In the meantime, Livingstone returned, already very late, to Kolobeng, and made his report on the venture to the LMS. He had broken their rules in making the trip without their permission or even knowledge, and yet knew that by publishing his account of the British discovery of Ngami they would gain publicity that could be financially invaluable. He expressed enormous gratitude to Oswell and Murray, saying that they had financed the expedition and were "present at the discovery" but he insisted that it would have been impossible without himself. Fortunately another way in which Oswell was unlike Livingstone was that he had no ambition or sense of his own importance, and was perfectly happy for Livingstone to take the prize. Literally so: the Royal Geographic Society awarded Livingstone a twenty-five guinea royal award. "It is from the Queen," David wrote to his parents. "You must be very loyal, all of you. Next time she comes your way, shout till you are hoarse."

The LMS inspector Joseph Freeman visited Kolobeng in late 1849 and reported sadly that the Bakwena were "nearly all heathen, dressed in their native karosses [skins], their hair greased, necks belaboured with chains and ornaments, and many of them begrimed with red ochre." He concluded that Livingstone would need "a large supply of the patience of hope".

Sechele listened avidly to Livingstone's stories of the north. Sebitwane's Makololo had been part of the "Manatee" armies that had terrorized the southern tribes years before. They were related to the Bakwena, and though they had attacked the Bakwena back then, Sebitwane had ordered that young Sechele and his brothers be spared, and treated Sechele after he was injured, saving his life. Sechele had sent Sebitwane a present with Livingstone's first expedition to the lake, which had failed to get through. The second time, he decided to come himself.

Oswell arrived at Kolobeng in May 1850 to discover that, incredibly, Livingstone had left without him a month before, taking Sechele, Mary, and their three children. Mary was five months pregnant. Livingstone talked vaguely afterwards of "some mistake" in the arrangement, but, as Oswell's son saw it, he had simply been "unable to resist the desire and opportunity of being the first to visit Sebitoané". As it turned out, the boat that Oswell had brought 570 miles from Colesberg had buckled in the heat and was ruined. He went hunting.

The Livingstones, Sechele and their helpers visited the Bamangwato, and found that Sekomi had given up trying to stop them crossing the desert. "You beat me," he told Livingstone, "and I applaud you." With the help of the Bakalahari, they reached the Zouga and crossed it straightaway before following it to the Tamunakle. There they found that the Batawana had also relented and acquiesced to their plans to go north to the Makololo. Chief Lechulatebe supplied guides to take them up the river, but also warned that it swarmed with tsetse fly so their oxen would not survive the journey. Sechele had not heard from Sebitwane whether he would be welcome there, so it was decided that Livingstone would go alone, leaving oxen, family and Bakwenas with the Batawana. Livingstone delayed leaving for a week to show his family Lake Ngami, but the visitors immediately started to show signs of malaria, including Robert and Agnes Livingstone. Luckily David had quinine with him, which he had heard could be effective against tropical fever. He gave his children an experimental prescription of quinine with jalap, rhubarb and calomel as laxatives. The dosage proved right, and the children were saved, though for a long time they were too weak to stand. He decided it was not safe to leave the family there, and so after "two very pleasant Sundays" turned back to Kolobeng. Oswell, not offended by having been left behind, came to meet them with £40 worth of supplies for them.

Thanks to David's disappointment and an overdue labour, Mary gave birth to her fourth child, Elizabeth, in August 1850 in their home in Kolobeng rather than on Ngami or in the Kalahari. Mercifully, considering the journey Mary had endured in the later stages of her pregnancy, the baby seemed fit and well. But the town was seized with an epidemic of pleurisy, and Elizabeth succumbed. "At one o'clock," David wrote to Moffat on 18 September, "she opened her beautiful eyes and screamed with a great effort to make her lungs work, and instantly expired. That scream went to our hearts, and will probably not be forgotten in eternity." In his journal, he said placidly, "It was the first death in our family, but just as likely to have happened had we remained at home, and we have now one of our number in heaven."

By that time, David was already planning his next venture north, at the first opportunity, this time taking a whole year. Before Elizabeth died, Mary had said she would stay in Kolobeng, but now she insisted on coming with him, along with the children. She herself fell ill, suffering pains, shivering and the paralysis of half of her face. Mary's mother was shocked and angry to hear that David planned to take the family with him again, and wanted them to come to Kuruman instead, but he refused even to talk about it.

Finally, in the Livingstones' fifth season with the Bakwena, the rain came, but even that did not seem to help anyone. "The crops look more miserable than ever we saw them," Livingstone told his father-in-law. "The soil does not retain the moisture. Most of the people look extremely wretched, and the dreary prospect before them is enough to make them run away." "All is dead and stagnant," he told another correspondent, "the fields burned up. The grass crumbles in the hand like powder."

Sechele picked a new spot to move to, eight miles up the river, offering to build new houses for the Livingstones and Mebalwe at his own expense, but Livingstone did not have the heart for it. He was thinking about a new settlement in some fertile populous region beyond Ngami, perhaps with Sebitwane's Makololo, and he had reliable information that the Boers were planning to attack Kolobeng and enslave the Bakwena while the

British were too busy fighting the Xhosa to intervene. He told Sechele he would not need a house in the new town. Moffat criticized "Sechele's having been abandoned, just, too, at the time he required most the watchful eye and encouraging voice of his Missionary", but Livingstone was more interested in the north now than in the arid hearts of the Bakwena.

The Livingstones planned to go north with Oswell again in April 1851. By then Mary was pregnant, but David still planned to take the family because he was no longer sure when or whether he would come back. When Mary's mother heard this, she was outraged. "O Livingstone," she wrote, "what do you mean? Was it not enough that you lost one lovely babe, and scarcely saved the other, while the mother came home threatened with paralysis? And will you again expose her and them in those sickly regions in an exploring expedition? All the world will condemn the *cruelty* of the thing, to say nothing of the indecorousness of it." When these words had no effect she told her son-in-law that she was praying that God would stop him.

Instead of answering her, David wrote to the LMS to justify the journey: "It is a venture to take wife and children into a country where fever – African fever – prevails. But who that knows Jesus would refuse to make a venture for such a captain?" And to Sewell: "I cannot enter into all circumstances of the case at present but it seems duty to go. And were I alone it would not cost me a thought. But O my children. Am I sacrificing them?"

Livingstone's willingness to "drag his wife and children across Africa" has become the most notorious fact of his life, and not without reason. It was a terrible ordeal for them, and his cool wry descriptions of their suffering present him in his most unsympathetic light. There are several considerations to be borne in mind, however, before judging his conduct. One is that, as far as Mary is concerned, while we do not have her own words on the subject, there is no evidence at all that she went with David reluctantly, and some evidence that she was a willing partner. Oswell, paying tribute to her toughness and devotion, said that she "encouraged the prosecution of the expeditions" and that her nerve failed "on one occasion only – when her husband wanted to leave her behind", evidently referring to this very occasion. An early biographer, William Blaikie, says that "there were invincible objections" to Mary's remaining at Kuruman with the children, and since that arrangement would have been infinitely more convenient for David, it seems the objections must have been Mary's. For whatever reason, it seems she could not bear the thought of living for a year or more with her parents – and this idea also puts David's refusal to explain himself to Mary's mother in a better light. It has been said that David should never have married, but that is hardly the point, and moreover even that overlooks the fact that if Mary was so desperate not to return to Kuruman, she would surely not have preferred to spend her whole life there. Perhaps he should have shelved his hopes for a mission to the north to make life better for his wife, but that would have been quite alien to his missionary principles and there is no evidence that she would have approved of such a decision.

The children are a different matter. They were not willing participants in the expedition, and they were taken into inevitable hardships and serious risk. David was persuaded to bring them, whatever his misgivings, in the conviction that his mission was an inescapable duty and that his children's lives were in God's hands whether they were on the Zouga or the Clyde.

Chapter 10

SEBITWANE

The Livingstones and their crew left Kolobeng for Linyanti to meet Sebitwane and his tribe, the Makololo, in April 1851. Since they had visited Lake Ngami, Sebitwane had become the next goal in the European discovery of the interior, representing, as Oswell argued, links with the Zambezi, the Portuguese and the coast, and they hoped to establish a new mission station that would open the heart of Africa. Believing that his travels would now be of greater public interest, Livingstone started keeping the journal that he maintained to the end of his life.

Oswell went before the Livingstones digging wells, which made the going a little easier, but they still went days without water. Approaching the Zouga from the south-west as before, they met a Bamangwato man called Kamati, who told them that a party of traders – including Mr and Mrs Edwards' son – were also trying to reach Sebitwane and were a few days ahead of them. Livingstone was dismayed. Kamati told Livingstone that, in return for a replacement for his broken gun, he could take them due north instead of following the rivers, and they would reach Sebitwane before the traders. Oswell provided the gun. "God seemed kindly to reserve the honour of reaching Sebitoané first for us," Livingstone wrote in the journal. Whatever element of personal ambition there may have been in Livingstone's urgency, his conscious reason was a fair one: whoever met Sebitwane first would have the advantage in making an alliance, and the gospel ought to have the advantage over mere trade.

They crossed the dry bed of the Zouga and then the fifteen-mile wide Nwetwe saltpan, where their wagon wheels sank up to the axle. Kamati handed them on to a Bushman to take them the rest of the way, through thick bush, heavy sand, grassland, woods, then three days of desolate thorny scrub without a sign of wildlife. Finally they found a long path of rhinoceros tracks, and in the hope that they led to water the oxen and Africans were allowed to run to it while the British stayed with the wagon. "As is always the case," says Livingstone, "the children drank more than usual as the water became less, and their mother sat crying over them as she saw the precious fluid drawing to the bottom of the bottle. It was no wonder; we did not know for certain that the men would return with water, and the very idea of little ones perishing before one's eyes for thirst is dreadful."

Thankfully, they had found the River Mababe, and went along it by night to prevent their oxen being killed by tsetse. A Tswana guide took them across swampland to the River Chobe on which Sebitwane was camped and there they met a messenger from the great man, who said his kgosi had come 300 miles from Linyanti to meet his first white men and was on an island thirty miles downstream. Livingstone and Oswell left the family, crew and wagons, and met the great chief alone on 21 June 1851.

They held out their hands to him "in the accustomed way of true Britons", Oswell said, and were impressed that he instinctively knew what to do with them, but were amazed at the nervousness of the great warrior. In the middle of the night, he woke them by their campfire to tell them the story of his life: thirty years of constant fighting, his great victories and extraordinary survivals, how he had several times lost everything only to end up the richest and mightiest Tswana chief, and how he had longed to make contact with Europeans – presumably, Livingstone thought, to buy guns to defend his people from Mzilikazi.

Sebitwane roasted an ox for his visitors and said he would take them to Linyanti on the great river, which sounded to the British very much like the Zambezi. He told them their oxen would surely have been killed by tsetse, but that he would replace them all for free. While they stayed at his camp, a female attendant of one of his wives was brought to him. The wife had run off with a Bamangwato visitor, taking her ten attendants; the wife herself and nine of the attendants had already been recaptured and executed, this woman being the last to be brought back. Livingstone pleaded for her life, to which Sebitwane replied, "Shall I kill her after you prayed for her? Oh no." He then made Livingstone take him back down the river to meet Mary and the children.

Everything seemed to be falling into place for Livingstone's plan. They had been the first to meet Sebitwane, and found him eager to be friends, even ready to bow to Christian morality. So it was heart-breaking when after a fortnight together Sebitwane contracted pneumonia, which Livingstone attributed to the cannabis which all Tswana smoked, and died.

"Poor Sebitoané!" Livingstone wrote in his journal. "My heart bleeds for thee, and what would I not do for thee, now that nothing can be done? Where art thou now? I will weep for thee till the day of my death."

Sebitwane meant far more to Livingstone than the two weeks of their friendship would suggest. Oswell described him as "far and away the finest Kafir I ever saw... With a wonderful power of attaching men to himself, he was a gentleman in thought and manner." Livingstone felt so much love for the king who was going to open the heart of Africa to them, that it made him rethink the fate of the heathen in a way remarkable for an evangelical missionary: "I would cast forth my sorrows in despair for thy condition, but I know that thou wilt receive no injustice whither thou art gone. Shall not the Judge of all the earth do right? I leave thee to him." He envied Catholics that they could pray for the dead. The love that had sprouted up for him in such a short time illustrates how central he was to Livingstone's hopes.

Sebitwane's chiefdom passed to his daughter Mamochisane, as she was the only surviving child of his chief wife. Livingstone and Oswell waited three weeks to hear whether they would be welcomed by her – Livingstone persuading Oswell to break his promise to his family that he would return to England – and when she sent word that she would treat them as her father had they went on horseback, and finally reached the Zambezi on 4 August. Even in this weather it was 400 yards wide, the largest river they had ever seen, with white sandbanks, crocodiles and a hippo, and Mamochisane's beautiful town of Secheke on the far side. "All we could say to each other was... How glorious! How magnificent! How beautiful!" Livingstone saw a waterway leading to the east coast, and the key to the salvation of Africa. He could have cried, he said, "had I been fond of indulging sentimental suffusions"; but it would not have made a good impression on the natives, nor was it appropriate for a missionary to get slushy, so he restricted his self-expression to blowing his nose.

They did not meet Mamochisane because she had just given birth, but her representatives urged Livingstone to settle with them, offering to plant crops for him. However, he needed to bring his family to higher ground than this riverside spot to keep them safe from malaria. The townspeople agreed to move to a hilly region, but on reflection Livingstone realized the Makololo would be giving up the protection that the deep reedy river at Secheke offered them from Mzilikazi's repeated attacks, and decided he could not ask them to sacrifice their safety for his family's. He would have to find another solution.

They had reached the Zambezi and become friends of the Makololo, two crucial developments in Livingstone's career, but the most important result of their expedition, one which changed the direction of Livingstone's life, was an observation that could hardly sound less significant: many of the Makololo in Secheke wore European clothes. On one level this pleased him – it suggested a desire for "civilization". But where had the clothes come from? On enquiry, it turned out that slave traders (a tribe called Mambari, of mixed African and Portuguese descent) had brought them from the west for the first time in 1850, and, refusing any payment but slaves, gave the Makololo guns and chains to seize 200 children from another tribe. During that foray the Makololo met Portuguese slave traders from the east, who gave them three better guns in return for thirty of the slaves. They told Livingstone that the slave trade was repugnant to them, but it was the only way to get these goods.

This at least was how he described the situation to the LMS. He perhaps exaggerated how new the slave trade was in the region by a few years, and may have overstated other things too, but the crucial point is clear: Livingstone had met the slave trade for the first time and was determined to fight it. He was no longer just a Christian preacher or one who found paths in the wilderness for Christian preachers; he was fighting the greatest evil in the world in the name of Christ. This region, where the greatest tribe known in southern Africa lived near a junction on its greatest river – the point where today Zambia, Zimbabwe, Botswana and Namibia meet – seemed the place to drive Christianity, trade and European civilization into the heart of the continent, and deliver it from the slave trade. Had the past decade of sterile struggle been God's way of steering Livingstone to this very point?

Abolition was not an alternative calling to evangelism, but the perfect complement. As Livingstone had heard Buxton argue in London back in 1840, Christianity, commerce and civilization were allies, a rope of three strands to drag the slave trade out of Africa. It worked the other way too: the slave trade would fatally undermine attempts at social, economic and religious development if it was not stopped, whereas if it was replaced with legitimate British trade the new trade routes would give missionaries access to places as yet unreached.

The Makololo, Livingstone told friends and supporters, had demonstrated a demand for European goods, so why shouldn't legitimate British traders come and displace the slavers before they got settled? There were fortunes to be made. Had they not

seen ivory left to rot on the banks of the Zouga by people who
used it only for arm bands and preferred brass wire, and had they
not seen beeswax thrown away because they only wanted the
honey? "I feel assured," wrote Livingstone, "if our merchants
could establish a legitimate commerce on the Zambezi they
would soon drive the slave dealer from the market, and be
besides great gainers in the end."

There was the extra incentive for Livingstone that adding
abolition to his job description could get him greater support at
home. Thanks to Wilberforce, Buxton and the Clapham Sect, the
cause was associated with evangelical Christianity and so would
particularly appeal to his natural supporters. It had much wider
appeal as well. The government was thoroughly committed to
stopping the trade, not least because having abandoned their
own involvement they did not want other countries to profit
from it, while the British public were coming to see themselves
as the protectors of the world's slaves, an idea that combined
patriotism, justice and economic self-interest. Naval policing of
the trade routes had been expensive and had limited success.
Since 1807, the number of slaves taken from the west coast of
Africa had fallen only by about ten per cent, while the (much
smaller) east coast trade had increased twentyfold. The whole
of the slave trade from tropical Africa had risen by something
like fifteen per cent. If Livingstone could offer the British a way
of stopping the trade at its source, while sharing the benefits of
their society and religion, and making money, it would not be
a hard sell.

Livingstone's career had its second wind. He talked with Oswell
about settling down to start a mission station immediately while
the latter explored the Zambezi, but this brought him back
to the question of whether he should endanger the Makololo
by moving to the hills, or his family by staying on the river.
Unwilling to do either, he chose a third option: he would send
the family back to Britain. Now that Robert was five, the time

had come for the children to be sent back for school anyway, if they weren't to become "rank heathens". Once they were settled with the British, and he with the Makololo, in a year, say, Mary could rejoin him.

So they had to go to the Cape, and they had to go now. The rainy season would soon swell the rivers and multiply the tsetse, and if they waited till the next good moon to travel by night, the tsetse would be too abundant even for that.

So David returned to the family, broke the news of his decision to Mary, and on 12 August 1851 they started the 1,400-mile journey to the Cape. On 15 September, their fifth child was born on the banks of the Zouga. David wanted to call him Zouga, but Mary for once put her foot down, and they baptized him Charles after David's brother, but then changed his name to William Oswell Livingstone. David sent a lion's skin to Charles as an apology, and generally called the boy Zouga anyway. By others he was called Oswell. Mary suffered paralysis again, this time down the whole of one side of her body. One of the children had three attacks of malaria during the trip.

Whatever conversations David may have had with Mary on the journey are beyond guesswork, but we get some idea of his internal tussles from his letters to the LMS. He obviously wrote to convince the directors to support his plans, but did so with an untypical attempt at honest self-knowledge: "Some of the brethren do not hesitate to tell the natives that my object is to obtain the applause of men. This bothers me, for I sometimes suspect my own motives." His insistence that he never expected fame for discovering Ngami and "cared very little about it" is somewhat belied by his sour comments at the time predicting, wrongly, that Oswell and Murray would get the credit; nevertheless celebrity was not his overriding concern.

His other qualms were that he was abandoning the Bakwena, his family and his own hopes of a settled and calm existence. "My predilections are for a quiet life," he told the LMS; if that were true, his whole life was one long miracle of self-denial. The love he protested for the Bakwena also rather contrasted with the irritable tone of his earlier letters. But the pain of giving up his children was quite plain: "Even now my bowels yearn over them. They will forget me. But I hope that when the day of trial comes I shall not be found a more sorry soldier than those who serve an earthly sovereign."

As for the arguments in favour of what he was doing, it is not hard to sympathize with Livingstone's verdict that "Providence has not favoured our settlement at Kolobeng." Staying would mean hard work with little hope of reward. Going would mean a far bigger audience for the Christian message, and one which was not distracted by a constant struggle against starvation, plus the opportunity to stop the slave trade. "If I were to choose my lot it would be to reduce this new language, translate the Bible into it, and be the means of forming a small church. Let this be accomplished, I think I could lie down and die contented."

Two final considerations had to be raised with the LMS. One was that he wanted one of the missionaries further south to be sent up to the Bamangwato to pick up on his work in the region and "form a link between me and the world." The other was the cost of keeping his family, which brought forth a remarkable piece of rhetorical arm-twisting:

> Should you not feel yourselves justified in incurring
> the expense of their support in England, I shall feel
> called upon to renounce the hope of carrying the
> gospel into that country, and labour among those who
> live in a more healthy country, viz. the Bakwains.
> But stay, I am not sure. So powerfully convinced am
> I that it is the will of the Lord I should, I will go, no
> matter who opposes. But from you I expect nothing
> but encouragement. [8]

Chapter 11

"ORPHANING MY CHILDREN"

Having taken maternity leave on the Zouga and stayed with the family in Kuruman, the Livingstones arrived in Cape Town in March 1852. David found it hard to adjust to white society. He was nervous walking down his first flight of stairs in a decade, and when he preached he struggled to find the right English words. He had the uvula cut from his throat, as it had long troubled him – he had asked Moffat to do it, who got as far as taking a pair of scissors in hand but could not go through with the operation. They met up with Oswell, who spent £170 on them, including dressing Mary and the children in decent clothes. David met the Astronomer Royal and learned from him how to measure latitude and longitude, so from now on he could accurately map the territory he explored, making his travels more geographically useful.

David wrote a pamphlet there, taking the side of the Xhosa in their latest war against British colonists. He passionately supported their right to fight for their freedom: "We are no advocates for war but we would prefer perpetual war to perpetual slavery. No nation ever secured liberty without fighting for it. And every nation on earth worthy of freedom is ready to shed its blood in its defence. We sympathise with the Caffres; we side with the weak against the strong." He did not get a publisher for his controversial opinions.

The family sailed on 23 April. David, not having heard yet whether the LMS approved of his plans and would support his family, wrote the directors another strongly worded letter, saying that his children were made "absolutely vagabonds" by his mission, so those who sent him had a duty to provide for them. He also passed on the news that Sechele, in his absence, had killed an Englishman in retribution for murdering one of his own people, and was therefore not a Christian. The mission in that region had therefore not had a single success, and the reason God had withheld his blessing was that Edwards and Inglis lived nearby.

In May he wrote to his family:

My Dear Robert
Here is a little letter for yourself. I am writing it in the house in which you and I lived when we were all at the Cape. Do you remember the last time I saw you when you were looking out of the window of the ship and I was sailing away from you in the boat? You went away with Mamma to England and I hope Jesus has taken you safely all the way to England. I don't know yet but you must write me a letter and tell me. I am very sorry. I shall not see you again. You know I loved you very much. I like or love you still. Do you love me? Do you remember me sometimes? You may remember me but you need not call me your Papa any more. Jesus is your Papa. You must take him for your Papa. He is always near you and he loves you. Jesus lent you to me and now when I part with you for at least many long years. I have given you back to him again. Love him, for you belong to him you don't belong to the Devil or to the world. You must be on his side. Never be ashamed of him or of his people or of his kingdom. Love and speak kindly to Mamma and Agnes and Thomas Steele and Zouga. Never vex or be naughty to any of them – for Jesus who died that your sins might be forgiven does not like naughtiness.
I shall soon leave Cape Town and go away back to Sebitoane's country. Goodbye.
*   D. Livingston* [9]

To Mary, he said, "How I miss you now, and the dear children! My heart yearns incessantly over you… I never show all my feelings;

but I can truly say, my dearest, that I loved you when I married you, and the longer I lived with you, I loved you the better."

Livingstone waited in Cape Town until he heard from the LMS in late May. They were thrilled about his going north, promised £120 a year for the family, and gave him £150 to help him through his financial straits. In return, they insisted that he take a companion to the Zambezi with him, suggesting Ashton, and asked Livingstone to keep a journal for the Royal Geographical Society. Livingstone refused the first, saying Ashton would never go where there was malaria, and that no one else would be of any use; as for the journal – which in fact he kept assiduously – he said he could make no commitment.

Livingstone planned to visit Sechele and Mebalwe for a fortnight in Kolobeng, as well as collecting his books, medical equipment, etc., but first had to stay in Kuruman throughout September replacing a broken wagon wheel. There he heard what had happened at Mabotsa. In August, the Boers demanded slave labour from the Bakgatla and Chief Mosealele refused. The Boers warned Edwards to leave, so he went – "bursting into a roaring boo-hoo", according to Livingstone – to stay with Inglis, both men sending their families back to Britain, while Moscalele and his inner circle were given refuge by Sechele. The Boers then attacked Mabotsa, took it over and made slaves of the Bakgatla, killing 120 men and women.

While Livingstone was at Kuruman, the Boers moved on to the Bakwena at Kolobeng. Sechele told the story in a letter to Moffat (translated by Livingstone):

I am undone by the Boers, who attacked me, though I had no guilt with them. They demanded that I should be in their kingdom, and I refused. They demanded that I should prevent the English and Griquas from passing (northward). I replied, these are my friends, and I can prevent no one (of them). They came on Saturday, and I besought them not to fight on Sunday, and they assented. They began on Monday morning at twilight, and fired with all their

*might, and burned the town with fire, and scattered us. They
killed sixty of my people, and captured women, and children, and
men... They took all the cattle and all the goods of the Bakwains;
and the house of Livingstone they plundered, taking away all his
goods... Of the Boers were killed twenty-eight.* [10, 11]

Sechele does not mention that the Boers attended Mebalwe's
church service before sacking the town. A visitor in November,
the explorer James Chapman, said pages from hundreds of
Tswana Bibles were still scattered for a mile around.

Livingstone, who had declared Sechele apostate for executing
an English murderer, wrote, "You will hear of my Bakwains yet,
they are not broken-spirited Hottentots. That attack sealed many
Boers' doom." He told the LMS that it was the influence of the
gospel that had made the Bakwenas fight bravely in contrast to
all the other tribes who had run from the Boers, adding that
they could have attacked when the Boers were still setting up
camp, but Mebalwe persuaded them not to spill first blood;
"and thence arose all the subsequent success of the Boers."

Livingstone heard from survivors that the Commandant was
disappointed not to be able to behead him (Livingstone), and
concluded the broken wheel that kept him in Kuruman had been
God's way of saving him for the work ahead. He even concluded
that "the destruction of my property was a fortunate thing for
me": not only would he travel lighter, but there was no way
anyone could think all white people were the same, the Boers
having advertised the enmity between them and the missionaries
unmistakeably. And loath as Livingstone was to admit it, they
confirmed this enmity by expelling Edwards and Inglis from the
region when they protested against the enslavement of Bakwena
and Bakgatla children.

The Boers claimed the Bakwena had 500 guns and accused
Livingstone of arming them. While modern writers have
dismissed the figure, some have accepted the second point.
There is no evidence at all that Livingstone ran guns, only that

he mended them and approved of the Bakwena having them, points which he made no secret of. He categorically denied providing them, telling the *Cape Town Mail*: "… if you can prove that I either *lent* or *sold* or *gave* a gun or anything else but a *black pot*, and a handful of salt to Sechele I shall willingly leave the country." In 1850, before the matter became controversial, when his parents and sisters questioned whether the tribe should have guns, he wrote, "I had no hand in procuring the guns of the Bakwains, but felt very pleased when they did get them… Resistance to such tyrants and murderers [as the Boers] is I think obedience to God."

Livingstone briefly met Sechele, who was going to the Cape Colony to ask the governor to intervene against the Boers, and he asked Livingstone to accompany him. Livingstone said Sechele would get nothing from the governor, who was off fighting the Sotho. Sechele responded, "I will go to the Queen," to which Livingstone had no answer, except that he would not come with him. Sechele continued on his way, but was denied permission to sail and sent back.

Leaving Kuruman in December 1852, Livingstone visited what was left of the Bakwena on his way north, making a list of 123 children enslaved by the Boers. The greatest impediment he found to travelling at this time of year was flooded rivers, wide and flanked with impenetrable reeds. It sometimes took days to find a passage, and he had to leave behind the less hardy members of his crew. All but Livingstone himself and one other caught malaria, but all survived. If he noticed his fortieth birthday at all in March 1853, he did not mark it. He reached the Makololo in 1853 to find that they had another new kgosi, Mamochisane having stepped down in favour of her eighteen-year-old half-brother Sekeletu, and that Livingstone was still very much in favour. The Makololo had planted crops for him, Sekeletu had sent search parties to escort him when he heard he was coming, and on his arrival Sekeletu's herald proclaimed, "Don't I see the white man? Don't I see the comrade of Sebitwane? Don't I see the father of Sekeletu? We want sleep [i.e. peace]. Give your son sleep, my lord."

For two months, Livingstone led Christian services at Linyanti before audiences of up to 700, but was disappointed to find the Makololo no readier to think like European Christians than the Bakwena. They expected his presence to make them rich, they wanted him to teach them how to pray to Jesus for material and political gain rather than the subtler benefits of atonement and sanctification, and they tried to use his medicines as magic. He offered to teach reading, but Sekeletu politely refused. He had heard about Sechele and was afraid "lest it should change his heart and make him content with one wife".

Livingstone had not wanted to stay nearly so long at Linyanti. Though it sits incongruously with his decision to send his family to Britain to avoid making the Makololo move away from the river, his plan was to tour the region to find a fever-free spot for a mission station as soon as possible. He delayed because Sekeletu insisted he had not had a good enough look at him, and then decided to accompany him, which meant lengthy negotiations with his elders, and then a crew of 160 had to be prepared. After which, Livingstone finally went down with malaria. He tried Tswana remedies, which did not impress him, and beat the fever himself with a combination of his quinine pills and "a merry heart".

They left in July 1853 on a nine-week tour, going 300 miles up the Zambezi, but they found no site free from malaria and Livingstone suffered seven recurrences of the disease during the trip. "We must brave the fever," he reported to the LMS. "It is God, not the devil, that rules our destiny." Livingstone unwittingly foiled an assassination attempt on Sekeletu by a rival chief, by standing between them at the crucial moment, and was then appalled by the reprisals on the assailant's father and uncle.

Livingstone found his escorts eager to please, but they failed to do so. "Nine weeks' intimate intercourse," he wrote to a friend, "hearing their conversation, anecdotes, quarrelling, roaring, dancing, singing and murdering, have imparted a greater disgust at heathenism than I ever had before." He particularly hated their stories of killings in which they would "imitate the death cry of the victim, a fine joke apparently from the hearty laugh". They were "dreadful savages" and their way of life was "inconceivably vile".

Nothing seemed to be helping Livingstone to settle with the Makololo, and instead another idea started to pull on his restless mind: he decided that rather than establishing a new mission station now, his greater priority was to find a route to the coast, opening the way for missionaries and traders to join him there. Sekeletu liked this idea too, seeing the obvious economic benefits, and he gave Livingstone twenty-seven attendants, a herd of oxen, food and some ivory to trade.

Just before Livingstone left he found that most of his ammunition and medicine had been stolen, including his own supply of quinine pills. He assured his parents, "We are immortal till our work is done. If I am cut off by fever my efforts are no longer needed by Him who knows what is best." Nevertheless he sent his father a will, in case any of his few remaining possessions be recovered, adding, "Be a father to the fatherless, and a husband to the widow, for Jesus' sake."

The obvious plan would have been to follow the Zambezi to the cast coast, but apparently Livingstone heard that some Portuguese on that coast had tried and failed to make the same journey in reverse, so he decided to go for the west coast instead. He was offered an escort along the shortest route by the Mambari, the tribe who had bought slaves from the Makololo, but this would never do. It would mean going along a slave trading route with a slave trading caravan, effectively introducing himself as a slave trader to the residents among whom he wanted to establish an abolitionist trading route. So instead Livingstone was going to follow the Zambezi 400 miles north-west then head westwards across land for a thousand miles to the Portuguese port of Luanda in what is now northern Angola.

LIVINGSTONE'S COAST TO COAST JOURNEY
1853–1856

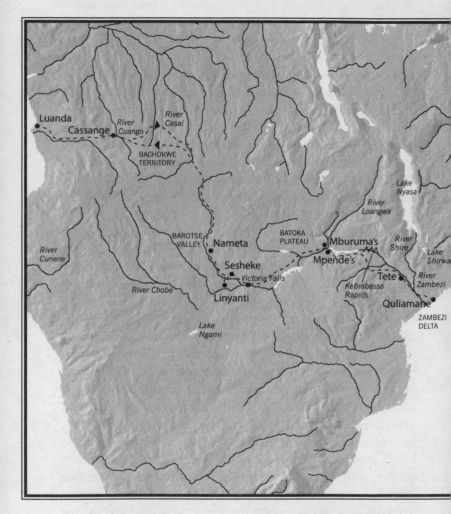

Chapter 12

A LONG WALK

After waiting for rain to deepen the river, on 11 November 1853 Livingstone and his Makololo crew paddled up the Chobe to the Zambezi, then rode upstream. His luggage included a one-man tent, two rugs, clothes, tea, coffee and sugar, three guns for himself and three for his men, twenty pounds of beads as currency, navigational equipment, a thermometer and a magic lantern given him by Mungo Murray to illustrate sermons with biblical pictures. The rest of his possessions he left in a wagon with Sekeletu.

They met Sekeletu's uncle in the valley of Barotse. He had recently raided the village of Nameta, taking nineteen children as slaves for his own people. Livingstone not only dissuaded him from leading another raid but at a meeting of the local elders persuaded him and others to release the children, and he sent his men to escort them home.

They were delayed by Livingstone's repeated attacks of malaria, and he grew weaker and thinner. Most of all they were slowed by the torrential rain. They were constantly drenched, had to cross river bridges waist-deep in water or sometimes simply swim for it, and repeatedly failed to move for days at a time. His guns rusted and his tent rotted. It made for a powerful, and at first favourable, contrast with Livingstone's parched journeys across the Kalahari Desert: "It was long before I could believe that we were getting too much of a good thing." Even here though temperatures were up to 90°F. The delays combined with illness and weakness demoralized Livingstone. His cure for his infirmity was to keep moving, so, when held up, "then fever laid hold with his strong fangs on my inner man".

He found the Balonda territory beautiful, populous and so fertile that crops grew easily all year round – "a Mahometan paradise". They were friendly, and every village had an idol – a wooden man perhaps, or a clay lion with shells for eyes. "When I saw their numbers," Livingstone wrote, "and thought of the vast multitudes there are in this land, all living without God and without hope, I often sat down with feelings of despair."

He always preached to the villagers he stayed with, and the magic lantern slides were a tremendous attraction – "the only mode of instruction I was ever asked to repeat" – but they failed to make the instruction any more effective.

Their hosts constantly gave them generous amounts of food. One chief also offered a slave, and another gave Livingstone a fragment of seashell, a rare treasure 700 miles from the sea. The closer they got to Luanda, however, the less friendly people became, being more affected by the slave trade and therefore both more suspicious and more brutal. In March 1854, they entered the territory of the Bachokwe and, after sending the usual offering of ox meat to the chief, found themselves surrounded by the tribe, who were armed with guns, arrows, spears and swords. They had their teeth filed to a point and made a tremendously intimidating noise. Claiming one of Livingstone's group had spat on them, the chief demanded the gift of a slave or a gun in restitution. Offers of a smaller gift only angered them and Livingstone, sitting with a shotgun in his lap, realized a fight looked unavoidable. Confident that his men, drilled by Sebitwane, would get the better of them, he kept to his rule of avoiding first blood – though he feared that he would be the first target. "One young man made a charge at my head from behind, but I quickly brought round the muzzle of my gun to his mouth and he retreated." Livingstone invited the chief and elders to sit with him, and when they did so his own men quietly surrounded them. Livingstone insisted they only wanted to pass peacefully, and, while ready to fight, would not strike first. After a long silence, the chief announced that he would accept an ox, which Livingstone paid, receiving in return that evening a few pounds of the same ox.

A week later, Livingstone had a serious run-in with his own men. He was suffering from fever when a dispute arose about beads he had given some of them to buy food with. Thinking he had sorted it out he went to bed. They woke him in the morning making a noise so loud it hurt him in his feeble state. Three times he asked them to be quiet, getting no response but laughter. As he saw it, they were taking advantage of his illness to mutiny, and if he allowed it the expedition would be destroyed by indiscipline, so he burst out of the tent with his double-barrelled pistol and told them "that I must maintain discipline, though at the expense of some of their limbs; so long as we travelled together they must remember that I was master, and not they". They never gave him any more trouble.

Increasingly the travellers found villages demanding payment for allowing them to pass, evidently used to taking a toll from slave traders going to Luanda. Sometimes they crept past by night. They gave up their clothes and oxen, Sekeletu's ivory and Livingstone's razors, cutlery, etc. Chiefs asked for men as slaves, which of course Livingstone refused. Finding that villagers refused to take an ox which was missing a tail for fear it had been enchanted, they cut all the tails off, but this only saved them enough for their own meals. The Makololo implored Livingstone to turn back, but he said that even if they did so he would carry on alone. By the time they reached their last great obstacle, the River Cuango, 350 miles outside the town of Luanda and a border of Portuguese territory, the only thing Livingstone had left to trade was his bedding, which he had kept to pay for the ferry crossing. But a tribe barred the way to the boat, demanding the bedding. When he explained he could not pay them and cross the river too, they told him, "You must go back the way you came." While Livingstone was contemplating that defeat, a mixed race sergeant in the Portuguese army from Luanda saw them and took them on the ferry with him, bedding intact. From then on they passed freely, though the locals annoyed Livingstone by telling his crew that he was taking them to the coast "to sell them all to be taken on board ship, fattened, and eaten."

On the last leg of their 1,400-mile journey, Livingstone's health broke down completely. The fever he had struggled against overtook him thoroughly, and was joined by chronic dysentery. He rode an ox but could not sit on it for more than ten minutes at a time. He was carried into Luanda on 31 May 1854, and taken to the house of the only Englishman in the town, Edmund Gabriel, the royal commissioner for the suppression of the slave trade. Gabriel gave him his bed to die in.

There were three British ships docked at Luanda, and the doctor of *HMS Polyphemeus* treated Livingstone with opium, quinine and calomel, and he was out of bed after two weeks, though he suffered serious relapses throughout his four months there. Only in August was he well enough to start writing letters and reports, and to take his men on a tour of one of the British ships. Having believed that their canoes on the Zambezi were the greatest vessels in the world they were beside themselves with excitement, and the food and respect they were given by the crew put an end to suspicions that Livingstone was taking them there as slaves. They worked for sixpence a day shovelling coal, or "stones that burn". As for the colonists, despite the fact that it was the British who suppressed their slave trade, Livingstone was impressed at how much better they treated Africans than British colonists in the Cape. Livingstone was upset to find no letters waiting for him and concluded that no one had expected him to make it alive.

He had achieved a hugely impressive feat in reaching Luanda, overcoming disease, hostile locals and arduous travelling conditions, and yet paradoxically that very fact made his expedition a failure. He had hoped to prove that traders could easily travel between Luanda and Linyanti; instead he had proved that even those who had the stamina to trudge through a thousand miles of steaming swampy forest and the luck not to die in the process would be stripped of everything they carried.

The captain of *HMS Forerunner* offered Livingstone free passage home. The proposal was attractive. If the journey from Linyanti had almost killed him, the return had every chance of finishing him off, and it was already more than two years since he had sent his wife away for a year. He turned down the offer, however. "It would be altogether impossible for my men to return alone," he explained, which was true; but there was a deeper reason: to return to Britain now would be to accept the complete failure of his African mission. As a missionary, he had preached for thirteen years and gained one convert whom he then pronounced apostate; as an explorer his attempt to open the interior had merely proved it impenetrable; as an abolitionist he had got no further than an idea. As a believer, he had a choice: either he could concede that he had followed what he thought was the call of the Lord only to find that the Lord apparently had no use for him, or he could give Providence one last chance to accept his efforts to be a pioneer in the campaign to bring the light of Christ into the lives of millions living in darkness and rescue them from their enemies.

And so, having failed to forge a path from Makololo territory to the west coast, he decided to take the last chance to salvage his vocation and try to open an eastern passage. On 20 September 1854, he turned round and started the 2,000-mile walk to the east coast and the Zambezi delta.

Chapter 13

TWO OCEANS

One hundred and fifty miles out of Luanda, while still in Portuguese territory, Livingstone heard that the *Forerunner* had been wrecked off Madeira, killing fourteen people. The reports, letters, journal and maps Livingstone had sent home from Luanda had been on board, so he spent six weeks rewriting them before leaving the colony. But what more graphic illustration for a man of faith could there be, that whether in the malarial swamps of the Zambezi or retreating to the supposed safety of Britain, his life was in God's hands? "Whoever seeks to save his life shall lose it", and in risking his life for the sake of the gospel, Livingstone seemed to have saved it.

Livingstone and his crew left Luanda well clothed, armed, provisioned and stocked with medicine, thanks to LMS credit and the generosity of both the British there and the Portuguese who wished him well in promoting trade with the Makololo. He had brought numerous gifts for Sekeletu, including a horse (which died before they reached the Cuango) and a Portuguese officer's uniform, complete with cocked hat and sword. An Austrian botanist in Luanda, Dr Walweitch, had offered to accompany Livingstone on the journey, but Livingstone considered it an attempt to steal his glory: "As it appeared evident to me this plan would afford Dr Walweitch an opportunity of availing himself of all my previous labours, difficulties, and dangers, without acknowledging his obligations to me in Europe, I considered it would not be prudent to put such a strong temptation in his way."

They reached the Cuango on 28 February 1855 and on 16 March Livingstone went down with malaria again. They were travelling in incessant rain, which became so heavy they got stuck for two days crossing a waterlogged plain. The only way to sleep was to scoop the mud up from the ankle-deep water into oblong mounds "somewhat like graves in a country churchyard", digging trenches round them, and covering them with grass. When they moved on through the miles of cold, wet grass, Livingstone's malaria developed into severe rheumatic fever, and they had to take refuge in the next village. "I was forced to lie by for eight days, tossing and groaning with violent pain in the head. This was the most severe attack I had endured. It made me quite unfit to move, or even know what was passing outside my little tent."

While Livingstone was recovering, his crew fell out with their hosts and offended them by striking one on the beard. Livingstone gave the chief a gun and some calico in recompense, but as he had repeatedly found on this journey, meeting the demands of the villagers merely made them demand more. He refused and left, but after they entered the forest beyond they were ambushed. The villagers fired on them but only hit the trees. Livingstone had been given a revolver by a British officer in Luanda:

> *Taking this in my hand, and forgetting fever, I*
> *staggered quickly along the path with two or three*
> *of my men, and fortunately encountered the chief.*
> *The sight of six barrels gaping into his stomach,*
> *with my own ghastly visage looking daggers into his*
> *face, seemed to produce an instant revolution in his*
> *martial feelings, for he cried out, "Oh! I have only*
> *come to speak to you, and wish peace only."* [12]

Livingstone told him, "If you have come with peaceable intentions, we have no other; go away home to your village."

"I am afraid lest you shoot me in the back," replied the chief.

"If I wanted to kill you, I could shoot you in the face as well," said Livingstone. When the chief refused to turn his back on him, Livingstone said, "Tell him to observe that I am not afraid of him." Then he turned, mounted his ox and rode on.

The incident confirmed Livingstone's opinion that villagers used shows of violence to intimidate travellers and had no heart for a real fight. He was heartily glad of this fact, because the idea of shedding African blood appalled him, and also because it fitted with his policy of impressing Africans with what he considered European virtues, such as unflappable courage. And as ever, being with one African people made him forget everything he deplored about others: "The negro character in these parts, and in Angola, is essentially cowardly, except when influenced by success... They are by no means equal to the Cape Caffres in any respect whatever."

They took a more northerly route from there to avoid the Bachokwe, who had proved such expensive hosts last time. One chief they stayed with, Kawawa, was thoroughly friendly in the evening, though terrified by the magic lantern pictures, but overnight he heard about the levy the Bachokwe had taken from them, and threatened to prevent them crossing the river unless they paid him an ox, a gun and a robe. "I replied that the goods were my property and not his; that I would never have it said that a white man had paid tribute to a black; and that I would cross the Kasai in spite of him." The villagers seized their bows and spears. Livingstone started to ride away, ordering his men to follow, but many of them were too worried to turn their backs, so he drew his pistol and ran at Kawawa. Chief and people retreated, and Livingstone shouted to his men to take up their luggage and march. Most of them did so, but one stayed behind, aiming his gun at Kawawa. "I gave him a punch on the head with the pistol, and made him go too. I felt here, as elsewhere, that subordination must be maintained at all risks."

When they reached the river, however, the ferrymen, on Kawawa's orders, took the canoes away to the far side until the price was paid – which had now risen to include a slave too. But one of Livingstone's crew, Pitsane, saw where they hid them in the reeds, and after dark swam across and brought them back. Villagers came in the morning to collect the tribute, only to find them decamping on the opposite bank.

"Ah! ye are bad," called one.

"Ah! ye are good," replied Pitsane; "and we thank you for the loan of your canoe."

Riding through forest, Livingstone was partially blinded in one eye by a branch. The quinine was temporarily damaging his hearing too. By June the plains were drying out, and they found one that had been waterlogged on their previous visit now covered in flowers, birds, butterflies and dragonflies. Nevertheless, while crossing it he was seized with yet another malarial attack. Before they reached the watershed with the Zambezi, he was vomiting blood. The sight there of the beautiful Lake Dilolo, which he alternately called "this little lake" and "the grand old ocean", revived his spirits, as did the remarkable discovery that the river he had followed towards it and the one he now followed southwards both seemed to flow out of it, so that it fed both the Congo and Zambezi, and therefore both the Atlantic and Indian oceans. Among friendlier tribes now, Livingstone covered the remaining 700 miles to the Makololo with no incident more life-threatening than being charged at by a buffalo, which he shot in the shoulder before falling on his face, and having a boat capsized by a hippo. He resumed preaching his illustrated sermons, and after one in the Narotse valley he made the following entry in his journal, remarkable for a missionary both in the assumption that the failure of the word of God is a forgone conclusion and in the hope that this will not ultimately matter: "A large audience listened attentively to my address this morning, but it is impossible to indulge any hopes of such feeble efforts. God is merciful and will deal with them in justice and kindness. This constitutes a ground of hope."

Livingstone reached Linyanti on 11 September 1855, fifty-one weeks after leaving Luanda. It had taken twenty-two weeks longer than the outward journey. The troop was greeted by the Makololo as heroes and "men risen from the dead", despite the fact that they had consumed most of the presents they had brought for them and had nothing in payment for Sekeletu's ivory. Yet Sekeletu was still keen to back Livingstone's continuing expedition, and offered him four times as many men for his journey eastwards. He loved his Portuguese uniform, and gave Livingstone a shopping list including more uniforms, guns, cutlery, a rocking chair, and a pair of green-tinted glasses.

There was mail waiting for Livingstone, including newspapers with eighteen-month-old reports of the Crimean War, and the news that he had been awarded the Queen's Gold Medal for his geographical account of the Makololo region. The latter was gratifying not only for its own sake but as evidence there would be support for his work from the scientific community as well as religious and political interest. But he was dismayed that only one letter from Mary, sent on her first arrival in England, had got through.

Livingstone wrote long reports on his expedition for the LMS, and put an extraordinarily positive spin on it. Luanda would welcome British missionaries and traders, he said, the cost of living was low there, and trade was free. The route he had "opened" was admittedly impassable by wagon, but was passable on foot. Yes, the Angolan tribes treated travellers scurvily, but this was because they had grown used to taxing African slave traders, and repeated experiences of being refused payment by gentlemanly Europeans would quickly cure them of the habit. He conceded that the climate was insalubrious and he had suffered twenty-seven attacks of malaria (though he asked the LMS not to publish this), but later missionaries would be better protected from the weather, and "no unfavourable opinion, surely, can be formed from mine, as to what the experience of one less exposed to the vicissitudes of the weather and change of diet might be.... I apprehend no great mortality among missionaries, men of education and prudence who can, if they will, adopt proper hygienic precautions."

He also wrote to Mary, explaining why three-and-a-half years after parting for a year he was still not ready to come and meet her. "I don't know what apology to make you for a delay I could not shorten," he said. "But as you are a merciful kind-hearted dame, I expect you will write out an apology in proper form, and I shall read it before you with as long a face as I can exhibit."

Livingstone left Linyanti with a crew of 114, led by the brave and resourceful linguist Sekwebu, and with a cargo of ivory, on 3 November 1855, accompanied for two weeks by Sekeletu and an additional hundred Makololo. On their first night they were caught in a terrific thunderstorm and drenched. Expecting a warm night, Livingstone did not have a blanket, but Sekeletu gave him his own and spent the night lying in the rain. "If such men must perish by the advance of civilization," reflected Livingstone, "as certain races of animals do before others, it is a pity."

Livingstone had long ago heard of the huge Mosioatunya waterfall a hundred miles down the Zambezi from Sesheke, and they reached it on 17 November, seeing columns of vapour rising from it from five miles away. They rowed towards one of the islands on the lip of the mile-wide precipice. "At one time we seemed to be going right to the gulph, but though I felt a little tremor I said nothing, believing I could face a difficulty as well as my guides." Creeping to the verge of the island, he investigated the structure of the waterfall, which seemed to be formed by the river meeting a canyon. His report, eschewing exaggeration, estimated the falls were 800–1,000 yards wide and a hundred feet deep, half their actual dimensions. He planted a hundred peach and apricot stones, carved his initials on a tree, and for the first time gave an African geographical feature an English name: Victoria Falls.

At the waterfall, Sekeletu turned home and Livingstone left the river, taking a shortcut across the Batoka plateau to the north. All the Batoka tribes they met observed the practice of knocking out children's upper front teeth when they reach puberty, explaining to Livingstone that they would rather look like oxen than zebras. Their way of greeting strangers was to lie on their backs stark naked, roll from side to side and slap their thighs, which horrified Livingstone. "I called out 'Stop, stop! I don't want that', but they, imagining I was dissatisfied, only tumbled about more furiously, and slapped their thighs with greater vigour." In one village he was accosted by "a mad savage" trembling in a "prophetic frenzy", with battle-axe in hand. According to his rule he faced him off long enough to prove his courage before telling the chief to take him away.

Beyond the Batoka tribes they found a large uninhabited tract, which he reported to be a "most beautiful district... which my people all magnify as a perfect paradise." It was good farmland, free of swamps and disease, full of fruit trees and unusually tame game, and the midday temperature was a "very pleasant" 90°F. There were remnants of an extinct Portuguese colony, but if they had failed to maintain it in such an idyll, he said, it could only be because of laziness. Livingstone's health had been much better on this journey from Linyanti, thanks partly to the climate, and partly to his decision to get his men to make shelters and fires when it rained, rather than simply braving the elements. At last he had found the base for mission into central Africa. Now all he needed was a waterway to the sea, and success would have emerged from all his years of defeat.

As they neared the Zambezi again, 500 miles from the coast, in the New Year of 1856, just as on the approach to Luanda they increasingly found local people hostile as a result of their experience of the slave trade. Livingstone was suspected of being a Portuguese or Italian slaver, and when he reached the last village before the Zambezi, which was ruled by Chief Mburuma, the people refused to meet them except in large bodies and fully armed, and Mburuma declined to meet them at all. The chief offered them only two of his canoes to get 115 men and their goods across the River Loangwa where it joined the Zambezi, and sent guides with them, who acted suspiciously, convincing Livingstone that they had been ordered to split them up as they crossed and kill them.

They reached the river junction on 14 January 1856, and set up camp. Livingstone prayed that he would survive to tell the world about the potential of the Batoka plateau for mission and trade, and for the ability to accept God's will either way, and he made plans to attempt a surreptitious night-time crossing. That evening he wrote in his journal, in a neater than usual hand:

> *Felt some turmoil of spirit in view of having all my
> efforts for the welfare of this great region and its
> teeming population knocked on the head by savages
> to-morrow. But I read that Jesus came and said: "All
> power is given unto me in heaven and earth. Lo, I
> am with you always, even unto the end of the world."
> It is the word of a gentleman of the most sacred and
> strictest honour, and there's an end on it. I will not
> cross furtively by night, as I had intended. It would
> appear as flight, and should such a man as I flee?
> Nay verily. I shall take observations for latitude and
> longitude tonight, though it be my last. I feel calm
> now, thank God.* [13]

In the morning, Mburuma's men, all armed, surrounded the travellers. They only allowed them one canoe when it came to it, and stood and watched while they ferried their possessions, then cattle, then men, onto an island in the half-mile-wide river, and then onwards. Livingstone entertained the soldiers with his watch and eyeglass, and was the last to leave, by which time it was clear there would be no attack. Wondering whether their apparent hostility had only been self-defence, he gave them presents, including some red baize, which Sekeletu had given him to buy a canoe, and they parted friends.

Going along the north bank of the Zambezi, and entering what is now Mozambique, they were increasingly slowed by hilly ground covered in woods and bush, and many of their oxen were killed by the tsetse. The south bank looked completely clear, but villagers refused to take them across, saying they were afraid of offending Mpende, a powerful local chief who was at war with the white people. They met Mpende's men at sunrise on 23 January: they were surrounding the travellers' camp and screaming enchantments at them. Livingstone refused to move on in case it looked as if he was afraid, and before long the whole tribe was gathered, ready for battle. Livingstone had an ox slaughtered – Sebitwane's practice before going into battle – but sent a leg to Mpende as a peace offering. Livingstone's men were delighted by the prospect of fighting, and carrying off slaves and women. "I believe," wrote Livingstone, "that, had Mpende struck the first blow, he would soon have found out that he never made a greater mistake in his life." Delegates came from Mpende asking who he was. Livingstone said he was English. They said they had not heard of that people and assumed he was one of the Portuguese, whom they were at war with. Livingstone pointed out his pale skin and long hair, which they agreed did not look Portuguese. They said they had heard talk of another white tribe who loved black people, which Livingstone readily identified with, and before long they were being ferried across the Zambezi, Mpende protesting that Livingstone should have come sooner.

Mpende then gave Livingstone a well-meant piece of advice: for the next 150 miles the Zambezi curved to the north and back, and was rocky and hilly, so it was worth cutting the corner, rejoining the river at the Portuguese town of Tete, 200 miles or so from the Mozambique coast. It was thoroughly sensible advice for Mpende to give, but that did not make it sensible advice to take, especially for someone who was testing the viability of the river as a waterway rather than trying to get to the end of it as quickly as possible. But they were facing heavy rain again; Livingstone's tent had rotted, his men's clothes had disintegrated and many of them marched naked. One died of causes Livingstone could not diagnose, and he was not feeling well himself. The detour would also allow them to avoid hostile towns. He took Mpende's advice. It was probably the greatest mistake of his life.

Their path was complicated by having to dodge as many villages as possible. Those they encountered made threatening displays which never amounted to actual violence. Livingstone did lose one of his most valued men, however, who left the camp one night and was never seen again, despite a three-day search. The route became a terribly slow trudge through shingle, long grass and vines, like "a month on the treadmill", and they had nothing left to eat but roots and honey. Just eight miles outside the riverside town of Tete, he collapsed and sent to the Portuguese commandant, Major Tito Sicard, for help. Soldiers came out to him with food and a stretcher, but after "the most refreshing breakfast I ever partook of", he insisted he had no need of the stretcher and walked into town.

He spent March 1856 in Tete, feeding and recuperating, only to go down with his first bad bout of malaria on the journey, along with Sicard. During his stay he inquired about the stretch of the Zambezi he had missed, and as he put it, "I was informed of the existence of a small rapid in the river near Chicova; had I known this previously, I certainly would not have left the river without examining it." This was the Kebrabassa rapids, the name translating as "where the work cannot go on". Livingstone had measured altitude throughout the journey by taking the boiling point of water, but somehow he had failed to notice that between

Mpende's land and Tete the river had fallen by 600 feet. If he had noticed, he would have had to conclude that Kebrabassa was more than a small rapid, and threatened, at least, to make the river unnavigable. And that would have meant the failure of his mission, the final disproof of the fact which Livingstone had spent three years of extreme hardship trying to confirm: that the river was a highway into the middle of Africa for traders and missionaries. It would have meant that his fifteen-year African career had achieved nothing. The mistake may simply have been the technical error of an exhausted, ill man, but even such a slip as that would have been uncharacteristic. Coming at such a crucial point it looks like a tragic combination of miscalculation, misinformation, and an unwillingness to face up to the death of his dream.

Livingstone left all but eight of Sekeletu's men at Tete, telling them he was making the briefest of visits to Britain and would return for them within the year. He reached the seaport of Quilimane on 20 May 1856. There the fever hit him dangerously enough for him to give his host instructions in the event of his death.

Letters were waiting for him there – none from his family, but one from the LMS directors, the first since he had told them he was planning this expedition four years previously. It was nine months old, replying to his report from Luanda, and he read it with a sinking heart. The directors went through the details of his journey to Luanda, expressing admiration for his courage and endurance, and offering "congratulations on the results achieved by your indefatigable labor in the cause of philanthropy and science", conspicuously failing to mention the cause in which they were employing him. Sure enough, they went on to say that they were "restricted in their power of aiding plans connected only remotely with the spread of the Gospel". They accepted that his explorations might perhaps ultimately allow mission to the interior, but, even so, the prevalence of disease made that a distant prospect and the LMS did not have the money for such demanding and speculative work. On Livingstone's expected visit to England they looked forward to "conferring with you fully on your future plans".

Livingstone was furious that his missionary society seemed to be dropping him at the moment of his breakthrough, but decided he would continue without them if need be. "The old love of independence," he said, "which I had so strongly before joining the society, again returned." The Makololo believed in him, if no one else did, and their society would be enough, though he wrote around asking if anyone else might employ him in Africa. He sent a letter to the president of the Royal Geographical Society, Sir Roderick Murchison, who had so fervently praised his work, saying that the LMS would probably withdraw him from Africa and send him to China.

There was another discovery awaiting him at Quilimane, a personal one but in its way as remarkable as any that he had made in his travels: he was no longer just another British missionary out among the heathen, his doings followed by a small group of friends, family and loyal supporters. Royal Navy frigates, on the instructions of the Foreign Office, had been calling there regularly to see whether he had arrived and to take him home. Livingstone was a very famous man.

Chapter 14

NATIONAL HERO

Livingstone took one African with him when he left for Britain in June 1856, Sekwebu, who had been his right hand man and an invaluable translator. The rest of the eight who had come to Quilimane were also keen to continue with him, not least because Sekeletu had told them to, but Livingstone worried about the dangers of the British climate and anyway he could not afford their passage.

The waters of the bay were deadly, and the first boat that came from the *HMS Frolic* to collect Livingstone capsized, losing all its crew. The second boat succeeded in getting Livingstone and Sekwebu to the ship but it was a terrifying ordeal for Sekwebu, with waves taller than the boat's mast and the ship itself being thrown about horribly. He got on well with the crew and started learning English, but fear of the sea affected his mind. When they docked at Mauritius, he climbed into a boat and threatened to kill himself. Livingstone talked him back onto the *Frolic*, and dissuaded the officers from putting him in chains for his own protection, because of the connotations of slavery. But that night he had another attack, tried to stab his new friend the chief carpenter, threw himself into the sea and, though he could swim well, pulled himself down by the chain cable and drowned himself.

News of another death reached Livingstone when they docked at Cairo. His father, who had survived fifteen years of David's African career, had died in February.

Livingstone narrowly escaped being wrecked on a steamship off the coast of Tunisia, and reached England on 9 December 1856. It was not surprising that Mary was waiting for him at

Southampton; it was more of a surprise that his ship came into Dover, so he had to take a train to London and back down to Southampton before they were reunited. He sent a note explaining his delay, adding, "Patience is a virtue, you know. Captain Tregear has been six years away from his family, I only four and a half."

Mary had had a horrible time in Britain. It was almost as alien a country to her as it would have been to Sekwebu, cold and incomprehensible. She and the children had lived in Blantyre with Neil and Agnes, but, as one might expect, they found her ways "remarkably strange", and they got on very badly. Mary took the children away and allowed them no further communication with their grandparents, who in turn refused to communicate with her. She drifted between cheap lodgings around England, lonely and ill, and when Livingstone was approaching Luanda, she tried and failed to arrange passage back to South Africa. She wrote a poem for their reunion, giving him "a hundred thousand welcomes" and rejoicing "the sorrow is all over now I have you here once more".

Livingstone found that the coast-to-coast walk which the LMS had noted so coolly had made him a celebrity. Edmund Gabriel had reported from Luanda on Livingstone's heroic trek across the unknown continent, which for the British public, as it has often been said, was in modern terms like a moon landing. Six days after he returned to England, the Royal Geographical Society presented him with its gold medal at a reception before a large and glittering crowd of enthusiasts, including the Secretary of State for the Colonies. The following day he was feted by the LMS at a huge public meeting to hear his stories and celebrate his achievements, which was chaired by the Earl of Shaftesbury, and they held a dinner in his honour. Murchison, the president of the Royal Geographical Society, arranged a meeting at Mansion House to establish a testimonial fund for Livingstone, and recommended him for employment to Palmerston's Foreign Secretary, the Earl of Clarendon. Also on Murchison's suggestion, the great publisher John Murray approached him for a book about his travels, offering not only to pay for all the maps and illustrations but to give him two-thirds of all takings, rather than the fifty per cent that authors could normally expect, on account of the huge public clamour for a memoir. In the meantime, his talks were reproduced in magazines, and the *British Friend* reported on "the extraordinary interest" of the public in his stories, and the "surprise and delight" of scientists. According to the *United Presbyterian Magazine*,

> ... *scientific societies, learned and venerable*
> *universities, civic corporations, mercantile leagues,*
> *ecclesiastical assemblies have vied with one another*
> *in declaring in the manner appropriate to each their*
> *appreciation of the services he has rendered to the*
> *interests they severally represent. Nobles of highest*
> *degree, philosophers of world-wide reputation, princes*
> *and prelates... have crowded the reunions at which*
> *Dr Livingstone was expected to be present and have*
> *sought to be made known to him.* [14]

The directors of the LMS realized that their letter to Livingstone suggesting a parting of the ways had been rather ill timed. They hastily assured him that all they had meant by it was that money was too tight at that moment for expensive speculation, but if it could be found, they would support his plans as ardently as ever. Livingstone was not a man to forgive that easily though.

They were still useful to each other, however, and while Livingstone refused to go on a fundraising tour for them, claiming his throat condition had debarred him from public speaking for five years, he put to them a scheme for a major extension of African mission. Livingstone, assisted by another missionary, would establish a permanent station with Sekeletu's

Makololo, while Moffat would be asked to go to Mzilikazi's Matabele, the Zulus who were their enemies, and promote peace. Livingstone and the directors debated the details and in February came to a formal agreement.

Livingstone visited Blantyre in January 1857 and cried to see his father's empty chair. On 21 January, he took lodgings at 21 Sloane Street, Chelsea, and started work on his book, announcing that it would be ready by Easter. It turned out to be a bigger job than he imagined and was eventually published in November.

For a 687-page Victorian memoir, *Missionary Travels and Researches in South Africa* is plain, to the point and readable. Some readers found it rather shapeless, simply relating one incident after another and throwing in discourses on Batoka geography and Tswana religion as the matters arose – and indeed much of it was simply edited extracts from his journal – but others found this only added to the sense of immediacy and authenticity. As one enthusiast answered those who felt he lacked "arrangement", "I thought one just mounted his ox and went on behind him."

Considering that it is a book about his own extraordinarily bold adventures, it is, in style at least, singularly unassuming, which again only made him a greater hero in readers' eyes. Understatement was in Livingstone's personality, but also in his interests, as he would not persuade traders and missionaries to follow in his footsteps if he made them sound suicidal. The result was the archetype the age was waiting for – the man who conquers a vast inhospitable wilderness for civilization in the face of countless afflictions and impossible odds, but doesn't make too much of a fuss about it. As the *Westminster Review* said, the author was revealed as a man of "unaffected modesty, energy, courage, and sweet unobtrusive piety".

The unobtrusiveness of Livingstone's piety was quite extraordinary for a missionary writing. In a short, reluctant and apologetic introductory chapter which Murray persuaded him to add about his personal life before Africa, he gave readers four sentences about his conversion and faith, before assuring them there would be nothing more about all that in the book. Though there is much about the degeneracy of African heathenism and the benefits Christianity would bring, he was true to his word. Considering how freely he expressed his faith in his letters, this silence was clearly strategic. Livingstone wanted to create as broad an alliance as possible between people who were interested in venturing into Africa, including those who were unsympathetic to evangelicalism. Though it upset some fellow evangelicals, Livingstone wanted to share with readers his vision for Africa rather than his faith.

More striking still for Livingstone's original readers was his unwillingness to make any mention of the fruit of his missionary work. Here he seems simply disingenuous. The real reason for not mentioning it, of course, was that there had been no fruit; but admitting that fact would have been embarrassing and would have detracted from his message that the region was ripe for missionary enterprise. So he covered the hole in his story by saying: "This book will speak not so much of what has been done as of what still remains to be performed before the Gospel can be said to be preached to all nations." The impression that readers took from this was that Livingstone was a successful but wonderfully humble missionary. *Tait's Edinburgh Magazine* in reviewing the book reported, "Dr Livingstone met with many converts... not only among the poor but among their chiefs", concluding that "Africa is the most promising mission field in the world."

The climax of Livingstone's narrative was his journey from Linyanti to Quilimane, with his supposed discovery of safe land for colonizing and a navigable passage to it from the coast. The Portuguese, through whose territory part of the route ran, would be thoroughly cooperative, he assured readers, and though their delta was prone to fever, a steamer would get through it quickly and easily at the right time of year. It would sail up 600 miles of waterway – which was interrupted by "a small rapid, of which I regret my inability to speak, as (mentioned already) I did not visit it" – bringing travellers to the prospective colony. This "perfect paradise", Livingstone reported, was ideal for cattle, corn and health, full of big game and huge fruit trees, a pleasant temperature, and "most refreshing to the spirits". The people of the region "are willing and anxious to engage in trade" and if provided with good cotton seed would be eager to cultivate it for a guaranteed British market, whose merchants would in turn protect them from the pillaging Boers and Portuguese slavers. "An effectual blow will be struck at the slave trade in that quarter." A chain of missionary stations of the various denominations built along the Zambezi would complete this synthesis of colonization, social and economic development, abolition, profit and salvation. And to those who feared inter-denominational conflict he declared, "All classes of Christians find that sectarian rancor soon dies out when they are working together among and for the real heathen" – which perhaps he justified to himself on the basis that the rancour which had been the main feature of his relationships with other missionaries was of every kind other than sectarian. All in all, he told readers, as he brought his book to its heady climax, the Zambezi was their chance to be a part of "those means by which God in His providence is working and bringing all His dealings with man to a glorious consummation."

The delay in publishing the book was partly the result of Livingstone's unhappiness with his editor. He complained to Murray that this man was emasculating and dumbing down his text, and eventually demanded, "Every iota of his labour must go. I cannot and will not submit any one comma even to his judgment." In the meantime a number of fake Livingstone travelogues were published, and Murray had to take out newspaper advertisements exposing them. By the time

Missionary Travels was printed, seven months late, some pundits said he had missed the boat and Livingstone fever had passed. This judgment was premature.

The first edition of 12,000 books sold out in advance of publication, and a second sold out before the end of the month. He eventually made £8,500 from it, nearly six times the total amount he had earned as a salaried missionary. Reviewers fell over each other in their praise. Livingstone was "an honour to our country", "a missionary of the right stamp", "no ordinary man", "one of the greatest of modern discoverers", "a brave, acute, large-hearted man". Like other over-achieving Scots he was granted honorary Englishness by the press, having "displayed all the qualities which we are proud to claim as most characteristic of Englishmen". Charles Dickens, in *Household Words*, declared that Livingstone was "as honest and as courageous a man as ever lived", adding that the effect of reading his book "has been to lower my opinion of my own character in a most remarkable and most disastrous manner... My self-esteem oozed out of me."

Livingstone was mobbed by fans in Regent Street, and escaped by jumping into a cab. In church, though he kept his face covered throughout the service, a witness said, the people "came trooping towards him, even over the pews, in their anxiety to see him and shake hands".

While Livingstone had been writing his book, a General Meeting of the LMS on 14 May had approved his plan for missions to the Makololo and Matabele. But his plans to find alternative employment had also come to fruition. Managed by Murchison, who was a personal friend of the Foreign Secretary, Livingstone applied in March to be British Consul to the African interior. His proposed job description was to make the Zambezi a commercial highway in cooperation with the Portuguese, and undermine the slave trade by developing African tribes as trade partners, providing them with cotton and taking on his first journey enough equipment for small-scale production of cotton, oil and sugar. By the time of the LMS meeting, they had provisionally agreed a salary of £500 a year.

For Livingstone this was a prestigious commission to do exactly what he wanted, on five times his present salary, giving him freedom from the LMS. For Palmerston's government, it was inexpensive speculation which associated them with the hero of the moment, and if it should come to anything would give British mills a supply of cotton to rival US slave plantations. British cotton imports had quadrupled and more in the past thirty years, and most of it came from the States. Manufacturers, and other voters employed in the industry, wanted not only to bring down the price but to become less dependent on slavery. The government's main reservation towards the plan was fear of upsetting the Portuguese. Lord Clarendon and Prince Albert discussed the matter with the Portuguese authorities, who responded with an assertion of their sovereignty over "Zambesia", but allowed Livingstone free passage through it into the interior.

Livingstone's treatment of the LMS in this matter has been severely criticized. There is no record of when (or whether) he officially resigned, but the first public notice of it was at their LMS board meeting of 27 October. This suggests that for months after he knew he would have another appointment, he let the LMS and their supporters believe he would continue as their missionary, then let them down at the last minute. That he deceived them for selfish reasons has become the standard interpretation, but another was given by the late Andrew Ross. He says Livingstone told the LMS of his decision to leave on 30 April 1857, meaning that it was they who deceived the public, raising £6,400 for the new missions on the strength of his supposed involvement. Reliable though Ross's biography is otherwise, no reference is given for the letter, and there is no trace of it in the LMS archive, so Livingstone cannot be considered to be off the hook.

Assuming he did mislead the LMS, the most likely reason is that he wanted to force them to go ahead with the new missions, and so did not pull out until they had made a firm commitment and raised sufficient funds. It is said that he kept quiet to protect his own reputation from accusations of selling out by taking government money, but that is unreasonable: the fact that his resignation came six months later than it might have done had no effect on his reputation. He is said to have saddled the LMS with two missions that it could not afford, but this is equally unfair: his delay helped them to raise £1,400 more than the projected cost. Still, if they had known he would not be involved they would probably never have planned the new missions.

Livingstone's announcement came as *Missionary Travels* finally went to press. If he had left it any later, the directors would have read his resignation in the book: it concluded by quoting from their fatal letter and the excuses that they made for it, and announcing that he was quitting the society for two reasons: his need to provide financially for an aged mother in her declining years, and his inability to preach because of his throat condition.

On the book's publication, Livingstone went on a five-month speaking tour, the rigours of which he complained about more than he ever did of his walk across Africa. He addressed mill hands, industrialists, scientific societies. Everywhere he went he was showered with honorary degrees and fellowships, the freedom of cities and donations to his funds. He wore his sailor's peaked cap with a gold stripe, as he had in Africa, and was described by one witness as "a foreign-looking person, plainly and rather carelessly dressed, of middle-height, bony frame, and Gaelic countenance, with short-cropped hair and moustachios, and generally plain exterior... His face is deeply furrowed, and pretty well tanned." Audiences were struck by his broken, hesitant, unstructured speech, which he apologized for, explaining that he was unused to speaking in English, but they found that it only made him a more compelling presence.

At Cambridge, he set out his vision in a speech that caused such excitement it was later published as a book: "Those two pioneers of civilization – Christianity and commerce – should ever be inseparable…. By trading with Africa also we should at length be independent of slave labour and thus discountenance practices so obnoxious to every Englishman." He gave a generous account of his missionary successes: "Among the Bechuanas, the Gospel was well received. These people think it a crime to shed a tear, but I have seen some of them weep at the recollection of their sins when God had opened their hearts to Christianity and repentance." He finished by talking about how nice it was to see the blooming cheeks of young English ladies after so long, and then suddenly cried:

> *I beg to direct your attention to Africa. I know that*
> *in a few years I shall be cut off in that country, which*
> *is now open. Do not let it be shut again! I go back to*
> *Africa to try to make an open path for commerce and*
> *Christianity. Do you carry on the work which I have*
> *begun. I Leave It With You!* [15]

He sat down, one member of the audience reports, and "there was silence for a few seconds, and then came a great explosion of cheering never surpassed in this building". On the inspiration of Livingstone's visit, Cambridge, Oxford, Dublin and Durham formed the Universities Mission to Central Africa.

Back in London, Livingstone quickly organized his crew for the Zambezi expedition and spent a £5,000 grant for equipment. He seems originally to have imagined it as another solo expedition, while the Admiralty proposed putting him in charge of almost 200 naval personnel, but he declined, selecting a team of six men, in addition to himself. On 8 February he was officially appointed "Her Majesty's Consul at Quilimane for the Eastern Coast and independent districts of the interior, and commander of an expedition for exploring Eastern and Central Africa, for the promotion of Commerce and Civilization with a view to the extinction of the slave-trade." He was elected a Fellow of the Royal Society and granted a private meeting with Queen Victoria, who was delighted to hear that the Tswana had often asked about her, and that when Livingstone told them she was very rich, they wanted to know how many cows she had.

Before returning to Africa in March, Livingstone wrote to the LMS directors, nudging them into action on the new missions: "I should be glad to be assured that the intentions of the friends in subscribing so liberally are likely soon to be realised." This has been described as "blackmailing" them into continuing with proposals they intended to abandon, but there is no evidence that they had any such intentions. He also made a rather modest offer of help for the new missionaries: "Should they come through Mosilikatse's country to the Zambezi to a point below the Victoria Falls where our steam launch will be of any service to them, my companions will readily lend their aid in crossing the river."

Five years after the mutual heartbreak of "orphaning" his children, Livingstone had been given a year with them, but he had not made the most of it, being too engrossed in writing and speaking. He wrote about this to thirteen-year-old Robert from the Zambezi in 1859, in terms that could not easily be mistaken for an apology: "We have had but little intercourse… While I was in England I was so busy that I could not enjoy much the company of my children. I am still as busy and believe that I am doing good service to the cause of Christ on earth."

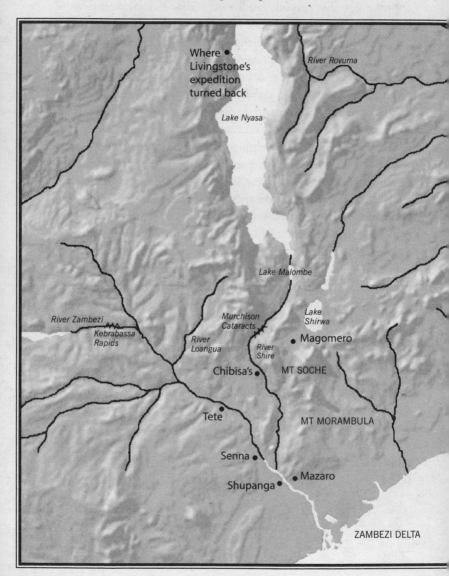

THE ZAMBEZI EXPEDITION
1858–1863

Where Livingstone's expedition turned back

River Rovuma

Lake Nyasa

Lake Malombe

River Zambezi

Murchison Cataracts

Lake Shirwa

Kebrabassa Rapids

River Loangua

River Shire

Magomero

Chibisa's

MT SOCHE

Tete

MT MORAMBULA

Senna

Shupanga

Mazaro

ZAMBEZI DELTA

Chapter 15

THE ZAMBEZI EXPEDITION

The Zambezi expedition left Liverpool on 12 March 1858, its members including Mary Livingstone and six-year-old Oswell. The steamer was to be captained by Commander Norman Bedingfield, whom David had met and been impressed with at Luanda, who had then survived the sinking of the *Forerunner*, and who was hoping the expedition would discover the ten lost tribes of Israel. George Rae of Blantyre came as engineer, John Kirk as botanist and doctor, Richard Thornton as mining geologist, Thomas Baines as artist and storekeeper, and David's brother Charles as photographer and "moral agent". Charles had been ordained in the US and applied to become an LMS missionary, but was not accepted, despite David's support. He resigned as minister of a church in New York State to join the expedition. They picked up from Sierra Leone twelve skilled African sailors, Kru men, to complete the crew. The equipment they brought included a lightweight 75-foot steamboat packed in sections, specially designed for the expedition and christened the *Ma-Robert*, the Tswana name for Mary Livingstone, literally "mother of Robert" following the pattern of renaming a mother after her firstborn child.

Kirk, a 25-year-old Scot who had served as a doctor in the Crimean War, kept a journal of the Zambezi expedition which is invaluable for two reasons. First, Livingstone's published account, *Narrative of an Expedition to the Zambesi*, omitted all controversies and failures and any mention of the expedition members whom he subsequently sacked, which left little more in the narrative than geography. Kirk's account, being strictly private, is infinitely more candid, and remarkably equable, though I'm afraid he pronounces "ten times the curses of Tristram Shandy" on anyone outside his family who reads it. Secondly, Kirk was the only co-worker throughout Livingstone's career to provide us with such a detailed personal record, so for once we can get a measure of how accurate his accounts and opinions of situations and people were.

En route to the Cape, Mary found that she was inconveniently pregnant, so David decided to drop her and Oswell at Cape Town, expecting her to join Moffat's Matabele mission after the baby was born until they met up with David's mission. "This is a great trial to me," wrote David, "for, had she come with us, she might have proved of essential service to the Expedition in cases of sickness." He wrote to James Young with more feeling: "It was a bitter parting with my wife, like tearing the heart out of one. It was so unexpected." Luckily, Mary's parents had come to meet them at the Cape and took the pair of them back to Kuruman.

The team reached the Zambezi on 14 May, and immediately discovered a major flaw in Livingstone's scheme: the delta was riddled with sandbanks. It took three weeks for the ship to find a path through the shoals. The ship was supposed to take them 300 miles upstream to Tete, beyond the malarial swamps of Portuguese territory, before they transferred to the *Ma-Robert*, but the water was too shallow, so it had to drop them after just forty. By then Charles Livingstone and Baines were both delirious with fever.

Commander Bedingfield and the ship's captain argued violently. Bedingfield outranked Captain Duncan but Duncan took his orders directly from Livingstone. Livingstone took Bedingfield's behaviour as insubordination – for which he had been court-martialled twice before – and publicly reprimanded him. Bedingfield wrote an official letter to Livingstone saying that if he did not trust him he should let him go home.

Livingstone seriously considered this, but they patched things up. Kirk noted, "I rather think the Capt. does not try to make matters go smoothly... He seems to have expected to live the life of a man-of-war commander, and has no idea of being subordinate."

They built an iron house for their equipment on what they called Expedition Island, put the *Ma-Robert* together, and ferried their things in batches for the remaining 260 miles. On 15 June they found themselves in the middle of a war between the Portuguese and the Mariano people, at Mazaro, eighty miles from the coast. Livingstone found the Portuguese governor ill with malaria, agreed to take him across the river, and sent Bedingfield back to the boat to get help carrying him. When Bedingfield failed to return, Livingstone brought him back alone. According to Livingstone, in the interval Bedingfield, frightened by the fighting, had tried to persuade the others to sail off without him.

The clashes between Livingstone and Bedingfield continued. Bedingfield insisted the *Ma-Robert* was not up to the job, overladen and already rusting. Livingstone believed he was deliberately running aground every dozen miles to make a point. Bedingfield wrote that it was impossible to serve a leader who did not talk about his plans. Livingstone wrote back saying that in his experience constipation caused by the African climate "makes the individual imagine all manner of things in others" and advising him "earnestly and most respectfully" that a laxative would be "much more soothing than writing official letters". Bedingfield said he would leave as soon as Livingstone found someone he preferred, adding, "In the meantime I will do my best to carry out your wishes as far as I know them."

Livingstone sacked Bedingfield on 31 July 1858, "...which he received", Livingstone says, "by dancing and singing." "Bedingfield turned out an unmitigated muff..." he told John Moffat. "I never met such a fool and a liar." Bedingfield made an official complaint to the Foreign Secretary, who ordered an inquiry, which cleared Livingstone.

This was the first of a long series of fallings out during the Zambezi expedition, none of which is easily judged. Kirk had criticisms of both sides: "Bedingfield was not the man at all"; he was used to commanding warships, resented being a mere sailing master under Livingstone's command, and had no patience with the scientific research of the team. He quickly tired of his post and did not try to get on with Livingstone. Livingstone on the other hand, Kirk said, was a bad communicator. He spoke to Bedingfield with undue harshness, and did not explain properly to anyone what he wanted of them.

Once Livingstone took over the sailing of the *Ma-Robert*, he was soon echoing Bedingfield's complaints about it, nicknaming it "the *Asthmatic*", and protesting about being overtaken by canoes. As the geologist Thornton had not yet found coal, they depended on wood, and cutting it took a huge proportion of their travelling time, so they had to add local woodcutters to the crew. The boat was repeatedly grounded, sometimes for days, and had to be dragged free by the Kru. "Very trying to their tempers," noted Livingstone.

On 8 September, the *Ma-Robert* reached Tete with the first load of equipment, and Livingstone was reunited with the Makololo crew he had left there in 1856. Having waited four times as long as expected, they were relieved and elated to see him. In Rae's words, "The men rushed into the water up to their necks in their eagerness to see their white 'father'. Their joy was perfectly frantic. They seized the boat and nearly upset it and carried the Doctor ashore singing all the time that their 'father' was alive again." While they were waiting for him, thirty of the 112 had died of smallpox and six were killed by local people.

Returning to the delta, Livingstone recruited two British sailors to replace Bedingfield: a quartermaster, John Walker, and a stoker, William Rowe. It was November before all Livingstone's stores and men were delivered to Tete, by which time Thornton had gone down with fever and Baines added sunstroke to his afflictions, having ignored advice to stop working in the sun.

Baines and Kirk recognized each other, and Livingstone and Rae, as hard workers, but were annoyed with Thornton and Charles Livingstone for not pulling their weight. All recognized that tropical fever struck its victims with lethargy, but the former group agreed that the only way to beat it was to keep active. Charles proved to have no aptitude for the difficult and still experimental science of photography, his only real job, so Kirk took the pictures himself in addition to his other roles. Kirk says that Charles's genteel manners made a good impression on the Portuguese, which he did not mean as a compliment, adding, "Most of us are not too particular about appearances when there is work doing."

On 8 November, Livingstone took a group upstream to examine the Kebrabassa rapids. He wanted to see if they could blast a navigable channel through the minor obstacles. For once they had a quick journey, which cheered him up hugely, until they reached the rapids on 10 November. "The Doctor changed his appearance completely from the first time he saw the rocks," wrote Kirk in his journal, "and in the shaking of his head we could see that things were not working well."

They clambered over the perilous quartz rocks which were "huddled together in indescribable confusion", in Livingstone's words, and he measured the width of channels and the rate of the water. As they returned to Tete, he confided in his journal, "Things look dark for our enterprise. This Kebrabassa is what I never expected. No hint of its nature ever reached my ears... What we shall do if this is to be the end of the navigation I cannot now divine, but here I am, and I am trusting Him who never made ashamed those who did so." He thought of the stardom bestowed on him in Britain in the belief that he would succeed in this venture, and reminded the Lord, "It was given for Thy dear Son's sake. It will promote Thy glory if Africa is made a land producing the articles now raised only or chiefly by slave labour."

Livingstone took the whole crew to Kebrabassa on 22 November, and had to leave the boat further away as the rainy season was raising the water level. Livingstone found he had herpes, while Rae had a fever. Heat, tiredness and malaria made them all intensely irritable. As Kirk noted, most of them openly argued with each other, and this was no great problem, but their leader, who was clearly worked up, kept his feelings to himself, making them "a serious inconvenience". Kirk particularly fell out with Charles Livingstone, complaining of his being a pathetic, lethargic dandy: "More than half the time is occupied allowing Mr. L. to have a snooze every half hour or so." While waiting, Kirk hunted hippos for meat, which Livingstone reckoned "good food, half beef and half pork". Kirk shot one hippo in the head five times without killing it.

After a brief detour to "discover" a mountain, which he named Stephanie after the Portuguese Queen, Livingstone announced he would continue with four Makololo and local guides to explore the rapids, leaving the rest of his crew with the *Ma-Robert*. Kirk said he would take this as an insult, and was allowed to join the party.

They climbed over large rocks that grew hotter and hotter in the sun, and on the first morning, Livingstone and Kirk in their thick-soled boots left all but one of the Africans behind with scorched and blistered feet. The three of them then, Kirk says, "spent several hours in getting about a mile further on. Such climbing I never had seen. We had to find our way among these gigantic stones, while every step was as if we should slip and go down some great crack out of which it would be no easy thing to extricate oneself, even with all the bones entire." The passing hours made the place so hot it was "like Hell if that place is what I imagine it".

Kirk eventually persuaded Livingstone to return to the Africans, and together they tried a different route the following day. The Makololo wanted Kirk to turn back to the boat with them, but, Livingstone says, Kirk did not understand their Tswana or sign language, while he himself "was not at pains to enlighten him".

Livingstone writes that leaping and wriggling over the rocks left their bodies "shaken and strained to a degree few can conceive". Sweat dripped off their eyebrows and soaked their shirts. Finally they climbed a 300-foot cliff, which was so hot they could barely keep their hands on the handholds. "If one of the foremost lost his hold," reflected Livingstone, "he would knock all the others down who came behind him." From the top, they saw the Morumbwa waterfall, and the gullies that meant they were not going to reach it. They went back to the *Ma-Robert*. Livingstone, according to Kirk, said it was the hardest work he had ever done, and Kirk quietly congratulated himself for acquitting himself in an African trek as well as the great man.

What was Livingstone to conclude from this experience? That the Zambezi was not a highway into Africa would seem a reasonable conclusion, but if he had been unwilling to accept the failure of his career as an obscure missionary in Luanda, the mountainous weight of expectation on him now as a British Consul and national hero would not make it any easier. Instead, he concluded it was merely the wrong time of year in the wrong boat. Reporting their temporary hitch to the Foreign Secretary, Livingstone calculated that when the river was in flood its level here would rise by something like eighty feet, "which must make a very considerable difference in the appearance of the cataract, if indeed it does not annihilate it altogether". The current would be strong and the whirlpools treacherous, but "we are all of opinion that a good strong steamer – capable of going 12 or 14 knots – would walk through in flood with ease."

"The Doctor gives a very favourable account of the rapids," said Kirk, reading Livingstone's report, "much more so than I could do." Writing to his brother, he was more forthright: "The River Zambezi is not the river described by Doctor Livingstone."

Livingstone, forgetting how annoyed he had been by Bedingfield's disparagement of the *Ma-Robert*, remembered that the Commander had inspected it in Britain and accepted it, rejecting a faster and hardier boat, the *Ban*. He asked the Admiralty to send the latter, or one like it, and made arrangements to buy it himself if they refused. In doing so he found yet another way that Bedingfield could be blamed for his problems: "B did us an immensity of harm by rejecting the *Ban* – we could have taken up all our luggage between 25 and 30 tons at one trip and then gone on to Sekeletu with all the Makololo." Instead they were left with the *Ma-Robert*, badly constructed, fuel-guzzling, the steel of its hull already worn to one-sixteenth of an inch in thickness, "the shabbiest engine ever turned out of shop."

Chapter 16

ANOTHER HIGHWAY

If conceding defeat was unthinkable for Livingstone, so was sitting around for a year waiting for a new boat. Another major river joined the Zambezi from the north a hundred miles from the sea, the Shire, so for the time being at least the Zambezi expedition would become the Shire expedition, in the hope that the river would provide an alternative highway into Africa that would allow Livingstone to honourably abandon the Zambezi. The Portuguese told him they had attempted the trip once and been turned back by the endless duckweed. Livingstone reckoned if duckweed was their only problem, there was no problem at all. It was, in fact, not the only problem.

He left with Kirk on New Year's Day 1859. The water of the Shire was deep and the *Ma-Robert* sailed through twenty-five miles of duckweed happily enough, before reaching clear water, though it was as slow as ever going against the flow with "an engine probably intended to grind coffee in a shop window", as Livingstone complained. He got increasingly angry with "this nondescript half-canoe and whole abortion of a vessel". They passed villages where the men pointed poisoned arrows at them, and as usual Livingstone overcame their suspicion by approaching them on foot and unarmed, explaining they were not Portuguese and not slave traders. But on the eighth day, after in modern terms crossing the border from Mozambique into Malawi, they came to a thirty-mile stretch of large waterfalls. This was the end of the Shire highway. Livingstone named them the Murchison Cataracts and returned to Tete.

There seemed to be little to choose between the impenetrable
Zambezi and the impenetrable Shire. Before going up the
Shire, Livingstone had sent Charles and Baines to Kebrabassa
to see how it had changed, and they returned to Tete now,
obligingly reporting that the Kebrabassa was as navigable in
flood as predicted. On the other hand, on the Shire David had
talked with a friendly chief called Chibisa, who said that not
far beyond the cataracts was fertile land around two lakes, the
smaller Shirwa, and the enormous Nyasa (now known as Lake
Malawi). While waiting for a boat, that had to be worth a trip.

Livingstone had hoped that the geologist Thornton would
have found a decent supply of coal by now, but repeated illness
and listlessness had prevented him. Now, after what Thornton
called "a blowing up from the Doctor", he went on another
excursion, and returned without coal and with "my legs nearly
covered with large festered sores" from scratched mosquito
bites. "It was three weeks before I could wear a shoe."

The Makololo, meanwhile, having waited such a long time
to take Livingstone back to Linyanti, saw that he showed no
inclination to go and grew understandably impatient. With
another journey in the wrong direction being prepared, they
told him that if he was not going to accompany them back
home he should give his brother Charles the job. David agreed
to this, but the Makololo changed their mind: Sekeletu had
commanded them to return with him, and they would rather
keep waiting than risk the penalty for disobedience.

Livingstone started his second Shire trip on 15 March 1859,
with Kirk, Rowe, Walker and fourteen Makololo. They found
the river people more friendly this time, and left the *Ma-Robert*
at Chief Chibisa's (towns were generally called after the kgosi in
this way) with Walker and Rowe, to walk for eighteen days to
the first of the two lakes, Shirwa. This was the smaller of the two,
sixty miles long and surrounded by mountains. Livingstone was
delighted to see the local people growing, spinning and weaving

cotton, and they spent twenty-two nights sleeping on the bare ground without suffering anything worse than dew. They had to turn back without seeing Lake Nyasa, but Livingstone had seen enough to revive his spirits and his hopes. He could forget the Zambezi and the Batoka, and transplant his dreams to the Shirwa highlands.

As they travelled back to Tete, Livingstone wrote to Lord Palmerston about the latest promised land: the area was accessible, fertile and healthy, ripe for trade and even industrialization. "The river rushing over cataracts is confined in a narrow channel and with very little trouble would afford water power equal to that of all the mills in England." He also reported that the Portuguese were collaborating with the French in reviving the slave trade since British cruisers had been diverted. In this he was perhaps reading somewhat between the lines of what he had heard from local people, but he was absolutely right. The number of slaves taken from Mozambique by western nations in the 1860s was to be roughly twice what it had been in the 1850s. Livingstone urged Palmerston that "colonization by our own countrymen would complete what your Lordship began in suppressing the slave trade". The Shirwa highlands were everything that the unreachable Batoka was supposed to be, a hospitable base for mission and abolitionist trade.

David also wrote to his son Robert, reporting somewhat prematurely that Christ "is pleased to crown my efforts with a sort of success that the world applauds", but that he himself cared more about the salvation of Africans.

They arrived back in Tete in June, to find the expedition in poor shape. The Portuguese, though they got on well with individual members, were increasingly uncooperative, annoyed that Livingstone had not disappeared into the interior but was trying to develop British commerce in their own territory. They also objected that by bringing free black men with them they "demoralized" their slaves. Kirk's response was, "We can't help

it. We must and ought to treat the Makololos as men," although
he added, "We don't make fools of them by supposing they
are equal to ourselves." Walker had fallen ill on the Shire and
persuaded Livingstone to send him home. Livingstone himself
was suffering from typhus and bleeding piles. Rae had had
several attacks of malaria, and though he had kept busy and
useful, he was sick of the expedition and planned to leave soon,
when his two-year contract expired. Rowe and Walker were
equally unhappy.

Conversely, some members of the expedition who had no
desire to quit seemed to Livingstone to have seriously let it down.
Here we come to a subject that has caused a lot of contention
between those who have written about the expedition. One of
those members was Thornton, whose case is relatively simple.
Kirk agreed with Livingstone: "his geological work has been
very limited indeed and he can say very little, even in respect
of the coal-fields which it was his especial work to examine
minutely." Thornton pleaded illness, but Kirk concluded it was
largely imaginary, mere "expressions of giving in to the feeling
of lassitude which all have felt". But while Kirk believed that a
good telling off had now set him on the right track, Livingstone,
apparently egged on by his brother, decided Thornton was
"inveterably lazy". He dismissed him.

The other person who attracted Livingstone's rage was,
despite his indefatigable and invaluable work, Baines, the artist
and storekeeper. His story is harder to unravel, but one thing
that is clear is that the stores in his keeping had not lasted well.
Everyone agreed Baines was not cut out for the job, though Kirk
added that Livingstone made the job harder by his own "utter
want of method in these matters". Baines had suffered severe
sunstroke and acted strangely as a result, though the details are
not recorded. He had at some point given food and drink from
the stores to Portuguese acquaintances. He had been painting
Portuguese portraits since November, which might be taken as a

waste of the expedition's time and supplies. Rae claimed Baines had stolen two shirts from him. Livingstone concluded he was guilty of theft, briefly saying he would excuse it as an attack of madness. He quickly changed his mind about this explanation and concluded Baines was merely dishonest. Livingstone got some kind of confession out of him, had him locked up and dismissed him from his post, pending further investigation.

Leaving Thornton and Baines in Tetc for now, Livingstone took what was left of his expedition up the Shire a third time in the *Ma-Robert* to Lake Nyasa in August 1859. Their one problem in getting there was the boat itself. The hull was so worn and rusted, the nearest they could come to repairing the holes was to plug them with bags full of clay. They had to bale out constantly, pumping the engine room eight times in a day. The funnel was on the point of collapse and had to be patched with sheet iron. The bridge of the boiler broke repeatedly. Whole days were spent gathering fuel to be converted into precious little speed.

One morning Kirk left the boat to collect botanical specimens, his main job, and arrived back twenty minutes late to find they had left without him. He quickly caught it up on foot and apologized to Livingstone for his lateness, but found that Charles had persuaded his brother to leave without Kirk and was now angrily saying he had just wasted hours of expedition time in sport. Kirk ignored him, saying, "knowing that the Doctor does not in the least participate [in] the mean feelings of his brother, I don't care very much".

Once, the boat was caught in a current and two Makololo being towed in smaller boats were thrown overboard and drowned. Livingstone, Kirk reported, was "sick from anxiety and vexation at the unlucky accident". A week later the Makololo stoker refused to work any more, and after admonition failed to change his mind, Livingstone beat him with a piece of wood. "He did not seem to care for it, so I dismissed him." Livingstone believed that strict discipline was always necessary to keep the Makololo on task, but this was a rare example of physical violence. That said, he gave Kirk permission "to break their heads if they do not do as I [Kirk] told them", on the strength of which Kirk beat a Makololo crewman, who accidentally hurt his hand, saying, "They never meant to strike me I know, but it is rather hard for a white man to stand an accident from a nigger."

The hundred miles to Chibisa's took them nearly a month. They left the *Ma-Robert* there with Rowe, and walked to Nyasa, finding more extensive cotton fields on the approach to the lake, and reached it on 17 September. It stretched as far as they could see, being 360 miles long and up to 45 miles wide, with scores of mountain streams pouring into it. The land seemed ideal. The cotton was excellent, and the people also sold banana, sweet potato, yam, tomato, chilli, amaranthus, pumpkin, maize, ground nuts, cassava and indigo.

Kirk, who was scornful of Livingstone's continued talk of steaming up the Zambezi, thought Nyasaland offered far more sensible prospects and would be a great source of wealth, but he was more willing than Livingstone to see the huge obstacle: the only known route was through Portuguese waterways, which they were hardly likely to open freely to commercial rivals. "They are fools to have let us in at all and it is what we would never have done to foreigners in Australia or the like."

The great blot on the landscape from Livingstone's point of view was slavery. The villagers they passed were terrified to see them, giving them the distinct impression that this was an area where slave-taking was rife. And sure enough they met a large "Arab" expedition (the Arabs being Arab-African Muslims from Zanzibar and the adjacent mainland) that had a great many slaves, and ivory for buying more – "the most blackguard looking lot I ever saw", Livingstone said. They had found one of the main slave paths to the Portuguese coast. With

Arab, French, Portuguese and African interests all involved in slaving in the area, it might be harder to establish a peaceful and prosperous colony, Livingstone thought, but all the more important to do so. As he wrote to his son Tom, "We think that our Heavenly Father has work for us there in suppressing the trade in slaves."

When they returned to the *Ma-Robert* at Chibisa's in October, it needed urgent repairs. Livingstone sent Kirk and Rae across land to Tete for materials, telling them also to bring Thornton and Baines back. Having spent their time in Africa so far on rivers and lakes, Kirk and Rae were completely unprepared for this horrendous hundred-mile trek in the scorching sun, in which the thirst nearly killed them.

While in Tete, Kirk's instructions were to examine Baines's store book and search his possessions for evidence of theft. He found a lot of art materials, but far from pilfering official supplies he had brought his own and supplemented the expedition's stock with them. Kirk could find nothing that he was sure belonged to other crew members or official stocks.[16] Baines denied whatever he had confessed to Livingstone, saying he had given away a few stores early on, but nothing like what he was accused of. The Portuguese denied having received anything from Baines – whom they liked a lot more than the Livingstone brothers – and Major Sicard told Kirk that he had investigated the accusation against him and found it baseless. When they met up with Livingstone on Expedition Island, Kirk told him the latest developments, but Livingstone was not inclined to consider blamelessness a sufficient excuse. He interrogated Baines, who protested his innocence and asked to be tried by the Portuguese court or the nearest British settlement. Livingstone insisted that there was no time, and the dismissal stood.

The role of Charles Livingstone in this conflict has been much dissected. Thornton said that Charles was jealous of him and

Baines, because they got on well with the Portuguese and got visitors and gifts of fruit, so Charles told tales to David in order to turn him against them: "he got spiteful, and set the Makololo to spy after all our doings indoors and out." Kirk admitted, "The Doctor... is easily put up to mischief", allowing his judgment to be swayed "by insinuations".

But from this basis, Charles has been magnified into a Shakespearean villain, driven by sheer arbitrary malice to destroy the expedition by turning his brother systematically against every member. This seems rather far fetched. David did not need such management to fall out with colleagues. He failed to tell people what he wanted of them, and when he had decided that they were no good he was stubborn, disproportionate and vindictive. Charles may have spied, misinformed and/or urged his brother to act against them, but it is not at all clear how much difference this made. Kirk says that Charles was "base, hypocritical, preferring underhand to open means", but also that David was aware "of his brother's insinuations often being base and false". By and large, Kirk's private observations uphold the complaints for which Livingstone disciplined people. "We have certainly been unfortunate in our men," Kirk wrote. "Bedingfield was not the man at all, he was a very incompetent person, Thornton was far too young and turned out lazy." His comment on Baines is far from confirming Livingstone's accusations of theft, but it is equally far from a glowing endorsement: "Baines was a very queer fellow. I don't understand him at all. He was very low, that's a fact, and for a storekeeper, quite incompetent." He also says that Livingstone dismissed Baines "chiefly on the evidence of Rae", who "acted... double" towards him.

Thornton, for all his alleged indolence, continued his geological investigations in the region after his dismissal from Livingstone's expedition, and Kirk noted his hard work. In 1861 Thornton joined the first attempt on the summit of Kilimanjaro, by which time the Admiralty had investigated his dismissal, and recommended that he be reinstated without loss of pay if he rejoined the expedition. They also looked into Baines's case, but upheld his dismissal. He spent seven years trying and failing to have it overturned, before returning to African exploration.

Rae repaired the holes in the *Ma-Robert*, leaving it with a total of thirty-five patches. Livingstone wrote scores of letters and reports glorifying the Shirwa highlands to his connections in Britain, including the Admiralty and the Prime Minister. It was "the finest cotton and sugar country in the world", "of unknown extent and greatly superior to the American". "All were delighted with the country." It was also a crucial point for attacking the slave trade: establish legitimate British commerce here and its success would quickly replace the selling of people, while the fear of the British would scare off slavers.

But Livingstone went further than ever before in the plans he promoted in his letters: he advocated not just trade and evangelism for the mutual benefit of British and Africans, but also imperialism. He had developed this line of thinking while back in England, in conversation with the Duke of Argyll, a member of Palmerston's government and friend of Prince Albert who had taken an interest in his achievements. The only other person with whom he shared the idea was Adam Sedgwick, the Professor of Geography who published Livingstone's Cambridge lecture. Telling Sedgwick about the Zambezi expedition and its geological and botanical dimensions, he added: "I may state that they have something more in them than meets the eye. They are not merely exploratory... All this ostensible machinery has for its ostensible object the development of African trade and the promotion of civilization, but I hope it may result in an English colony in the healthy highlands of Central Africa."

What Livingstone meant by "colony" was not conquest and dispossession, as seen in North America, nor the purely commercial enterprise that had been British India in the eighteenth century, but the establishment of a British population under British rule, with all kinds of commercial and social links with the native people, in order to have a good influence on them, morally and spiritually as well as commercially and socially, including the elimination of the slave trade. As he said in a letter to Murchison in February 1859, "I think twenty or thirty good Christian Scotch families with their minister and elders would produce an impression in ten years that would rejoice the hearts of all lovers of our race."

Now he was pressing this "glorious prospect for both Africa and England" on the Prime Minister and the Admiralty. "I feel every day more and more impressed with the idea that a colony of our own hardworking Christian people is the only means that will put a stop to the slave trade entirely – and render us independent of the produce of slave labour..." he wrote. "If you can do anything towards bringing the idea of a colony prominently forward you will perform a great service. I mean a Christian colony. A bodily transplantation of all our peculiarities as a Christian people and for a specific object, bending all our energies to the extinction of the trade in the bodies of men."

Livingstone also in his letters claimed the discovery of Lake Nyasa. He had met a Portuguese trader, Candido José da Costa Cardoso, who said he had been there thirteen years ago, but Livingstone tried to discredit him, saying he had pointed in the wrong direction when he talked about it, and mentioned lots of cabbage palms on the way, which Livingstone had not seen. Livingstone's scepticism was partly geographical jealousy, but also political. It was going to be hard enough to establish a British colony of Nyasaland on territory accessible only via the Portuguese Zambezi. If the Portuguese claimed Nyasaland themselves Livingstone's dream would drift further still out of reach.

Once his letters were written, for once Livingstone had time on his hands, so he planned a 1,600-mile hike.

Chapter 17

RETURN TO LINYANTI

Until he got a new boat Livingstone could get no further with the expedition, so, three-and-a-half years after leaving the Makololo in Tete, he decided that the time had come to take them back to Sekeletu. It was a job that needed doing, and it would allow him to meet up with the new LMS mission that had been sent to the area on his initiative, as he had hoped to do much earlier.

The first four months of 1860 were spent getting "the *Asthmatic*" down to the delta, at a rate of a mile in four hours when the wind was not behind them. They collected supplies and letters, including one from the Bishop of Cape Town telling Livingstone of the founding of the Universities Mission on his inspiration. They were sending a team of lay and ordained missionaries led by a bishop and equipped with a steamer. "This is the best news we have ever had," said Livingstone. The bishop asked him the best place for missionaries to go, and he invited them to help found his Nyasaland colony.

Rae returned to England, as his contracted service finished at the end of January and he had no desire to extend it. Livingstone turned the loss to his advantage by asking him to oversee the building of his own new steamer, which he was buying because he could not assume the government would send one. This left Kirk, Charles and himself to accompany the ninety surviving Makololo for the 800 miles homeward.

Kirk was unenthusiastic about the journey, fearing the non-stop walking would give him no chance to get any work done, and would contribute nothing to the aims of the expedition. Like Rae, he wanted to go home, but he thought the expedition needed him and that if it ever achieved anything he needed to be there to the end to get any credit for its success, and yet the journey to Linyanti only delayed that end. Despite all this, however, Kirk recognized that Livingstone had a duty to the Makololo, which meant that the honour of England was at stake, so he agreed to the journey.

Charles was rather freer with his objections. He said it was not worth the risk to their health, and when David overruled him he became resentful. The day before leaving, on 13 May 1860, they argued. Charles exploded, telling David he was a bad leader, "that the members of the expedition did not get orders what to do, and were always at a loss how to act..." in David's words. "All were willing and anxious to help if I only would have told them."

David was stung by his brother's criticism, but could not help seeing some truth in it: he had been reserved in giving instructions as a deliberate choice, "believing that it is more agreeable to men to do their duty in their own way". But he could not escape the conclusion that this had been a mistake after he had ended up sacking three of his five crew members for not doing their duty in his way, leaving him with a pair of men, one of whom had arguably been one of the least dutiful of all. Even now David gave his assessment of Charles to his journal rather than his brother: "As an assistant he has been of no value... In going up with us now he is useless." They quarrelled repeatedly throughout the journey to Linyanti and back.

A further shadow was cast over their efforts to take the Makololo home when, out of the ninety surviving men, thirty refused to leave Tete. The majority of the men were not ethnic Makololo but from subject people; many had married local slaves, and they felt they had a better life under the Portuguese than under Sekeletu. According to Charles Livingstone, half of the remainder turned back before they reached Kebrabassa.

Livingstone enjoyed being on the march again and seeing the chiefs he had met on the way out four years before. He found some of them rather more deferential this time: "The sight of our men, now armed with muskets, had a great effect. Without any bullying, firearms command respect." At Victoria Falls they found a white man from Natal called Baldwin being held captive by local people. Baldwin had heard about Livingstone's exploits and decided to follow in his footsteps, but once they had ferried him across the river the locals would not let him continue – apparently because they thought he was reckless and feared being blamed for his death. When Livingstone put in a word for his imitator he was released.

They reached Sesheke, where Sekeletu was, on 17 August. He was especially glad to see Livingstone, as he was suffering from a severe skin disease. Several of his headmen suspected of witchcraft had been executed, to no avail. Kirk and Livingstone diagnosed eczema caused by psychological turmoil, which they treated with a poultice of cow dung before applying more genteel medicine. The sores disappeared, but the doctors knew the disease remained and would reappear when they left.

Livingstone went on to Linyanti alone, having left medicines, his magic lantern, tools and books there in his wagon. They were all still there. Also in Linyanti was all that remained of the LMS's new Makololo mission, which was four unmarked graves.

The two sets of missionaries to the Makololo and Matabele had arrived in Kuruman in December 1858, shortly after Livingstone set eyes on the impassable Kebrabassa for the first time. The Makololo delegation was led by Holloway Helmore, who brought his wife Anne and their four children; the couple had been Tswana missionaries since 1839 and knew Livingstone. The other members were in Africa for the first time: Roger and Isabella Price and their baby daughter, and John and Ellen Mackenzie, who were expecting their first child.

Moffat was appalled by their plans to go straight to Linyanti and tell the Makololo to move with them to the insecure uplands. The scheme depended entirely upon Livingstone having made it up the Zambezi, prepared Sekeletu for the missionaries' arrival, surveyed the proposed site for health risks and persuaded the Makololo that they would be safe from the Matabele there. Moffat urged them to stay until they heard from Livingstone that it was safe, not least because if they left now they would be crossing the Kalahari in summertime. Helmore insisted that they had to be there when Livingstone arrived or they would miss the chance for him to introduce them to Sekeletu, and the LMS directors agreed.

The Helmores and Prices left Kuruman in July, the Mackenzies staying until their child was born. They suffered all the horrors of the desert journey that the Livingstones had experienced before them, but survived, and arrived in Linyanti on 14 February 1860, while Livingstone was preparing for his own visit. Sekeletu welcomed them as friends of Livingstone with the gift of an ox, but his friendliness quickly dissipated. He had made an expensive investment in Livingstone, on the assurance that he would return in a year followed by British traders. More than four years later, these were the first British to come, they had nothing whatever to trade other than the word of God, and they could not even tell Sekeletu when Livingstone would return.

They asked permission to live in Sesheke, hoping it would be healthier than Linyanti, but Sekeletu refused. Within a fortnight they had all contracted malaria. They had brought no medicine at all, though Livingstone had mentioned his quinine prescription in *Missionary Travels*. In the second week of March, two of the Helmore children died, followed by their mother, who had been deliriously hearing her children back in the desert crying for water. For the others, the fever passed, and Roger Price proposed that they should return to the desert and wait for Livingstone there. Helmore rejected the suggestion, but he died in April, and Price decided to retreat to Kuruman. He believed their illness was not simply malaria but poisoning. He spent May packing, when he was well enough, while Sekeletu let his people steal from the missionaries' possessions. When they were ready to go, the chief claimed one of their wagons along with all its contents – which included all their guns and both tents – which Price surrendered. Sekeletu rode the wagon with them as they went south, and demanded a levy each time they crossed a river, which finally cost them all their food apart from oxen and their bedding and most of their clothes. Nine days after they parted company, Isabella Price died. Their guides took them into tsetse grounds and abandoned them there – on Makololo instructions, Roger Price believed – so the oxen died. They met up with John Mackenzie on the Zouga in September. They reported the disaster to the LMS and were reassigned to the Bamangwato.

Livingstone, hearing Sekeletu's side of the story, wrote to the LMS directors:

> *On reaching the country of the Makololo in August last, I learned to my very great sorrow that our much esteemed and worthy friends, the Helmores, had been cut off by fever after a very short residence at Linyanti.*
>
> *Having been unexpectedly detained in the lower parts of this river until May last, my much longed for opportunity of visiting the upper portion was effected only by performing a march on foot of more than 600 miles, and then I was too late to render the aid which I had fondly hoped to afford....*
>
> *From all I could learn the Makololo took most cordially to Mr. Helmore. They wished to become acquainted with him – a very natural desire – before removing to the Highlands, and hence the delay which ended so fatally.* [17]

Livingstone later accepted that he had been misinformed, but not that he had any responsibility for the disaster. "Helmore did not write to me even," he told John Moffat, in a breathtakingly nasty moment, considering how much they were expecting and depending on his help. "I think they wanted to do it all themselves and have it to say that they did not require any aid from me. A precious mull they made of it."

Livingstone collected the medicine – including malaria pills – from his wagon that was sitting a few hundred yards from the graves, and returned to Sesheke, where he read Sekeletu a letter from Queen Victoria asking him to take the Makololo to the Batoka highlands to await British colonists. Sekeletu agreed, but it never happened, partly because of his recurring illness.

David, Charles and Kirk started back on 17 September 1860 with a surprising number of attendants considering the purpose of their coming to Linyanti. David's clashes with Charles continued, and Kirk heard David remind his brother of the "horrible, childish and utterly false assertions" he had made about fellow members of the expedition, "to which Dr L had not listened". Even Rae, it emerged, though he had left on good terms with David, was furious with Charles for trying to blacken his name.

Charles accused his brother of bad manners and having put a devil into him. On at least one occasion, Kirk said, Charles attacked David, "tearing with nails so as to draw blood and tear clothes, saying his brother was serving the Devil". To ascribe Charles's behaviour to madness, he said, was tempting, but too charitable. At one point, Charles was talking to the leader of their Makololo attendants and laughing with him, when the man said the wrong thing. In a moment, Kirk says, Charles switched "from laughing to kicking with iron nailed boots… Nothing but the high personal regard for Dr. L. avoided bloodshed in that case. The spear was poised and needed only a stroke of the arm to send it to the heart."

One hundred and fifty miles from Tete, they came to the village of a chief called Mpangwe to find that it had been destroyed, the chief and twenty others killed, and the women and children taken as slaves. This was the work of a trader of mixed parentage from the Portuguese colony called Sequasha, with a private army of slaves. He had offered his homicidal services to Mpangwe's ambitious deputy, supposedly in return for ivory, but then demanded instead more than half the tribe's land and their submission to him personally as vassals.

The aspect of this story that made Livingstone feel utterly sick was that Sequasha had followed Livingstone's path up the Zambezi claiming to be his "child" or deputy. In Livingstone's name he had bought ivory, canoes and girls at knockdown prices. The path that Livingstone was supposed to be opening for legitimate trade to subvert the slave trade was in fact providing an opening for the slave trade itself. Livingstone said in his *Narrative of an Expedition to the Zambesi* that he suspected this was the deliberate policy of the Lisbon government. Either way, his great dream for the Zambezi highway was turning into a nightmare. "It was with bitter sorrow that we saw the good we would have done turned to evil."

They hired and bought several canoes from tribes along the river, and these improved their progress so much that Livingstone was tempted into trying to shoot rapids in them. At the first rapids, Karivua, the canoes took in so much water that they were only saved because the Makololo leapt out to lighten the load. One of the crew nearly died, but was rescued.

The next they came to was Kebrabassa itself. The canoe carrying Kirk and two oarsmen led, and took the first bad corner well, but looking back they saw Livingstone's canoe being drawn sideways into a whirlpool, followed head on by his brother's. Distracted by their "almost inevitable destruction", Kirk's canoe hit an outcrop of rock and was flooded. One of the oarsmen climbed onto the rock, grabbed the canoe and stopped it from being lost; the other jumped into the water to lighten the load, and held on to it. Kirk was sucked under the canoe but pulled himself along it to the rock. The other two canoes were saved by the whirlpool suddenly subsiding, and Livingstone, having unloaded his cargo on the bank, came to their rescue.

Kirk and his companions had managed to save the food that was in the boat, but he had lost his clothes, guns, botanical specimens, notes, drawings and journal of the journey. Livingstone gave up on shooting the rapids, and they clambered over the hellish rocks and marched through burning sand instead. Within a day the Africans were asking to go back to the water. They met two large consignments of slaves being taken upstream.

Kirk described his appearance and state of mind walking back into the Tete in November 1860: "The shoes are through and the heels off, trousers torn up to the knees, one arm of shirt nearly off.... The expedition has extended over a longer time than anticipated and I have no desire to be any longer on it."

And yet, news was waiting for them that changed everything.

Chapter 18

FREEDOM TO THE CAPTIVES

There was a despatch in Tete for Livingstone from England. The government had agreed to his request for a better steamer, and a new one, the *Pioneer*, was on its way. They approved his plan for a British settlement in the Nyasa highlands, to be reached via the Rovuma to avoid the Portuguese. And best of all, agents of the Universities Mission had been sent to found the settlement. Livingstone's expedition was back from the dead. Kirk had found him very cagey when he asked whether he would be free to go home after the Linyanti trip, but now Livingstone asked Kirk to stay, and he happily agreed. Livingstone wrote to a fellow African explorer, Major Frank Vardon, "I am very much delighted with the prospect of a mission from the English Universities... The work before it is nothing less than the final extermination of the slave trade by the introduction of commerce and the gospel into the slave market."

They spent December trying to get their things to the coast in the *Ma-Robert*, and halfway there, on 21 December, the boat finally sank. Livingstone tried to make some amends for the deaths of the Linyanti missionaries by promoting his cure for malaria. He was struck by the horrible incongruity of the fact that while they were dying, he, Charles and Kirk were suffering the same fever on the same river, but found it – he said – no worse than a cold, and they spent only a day or two out of action, thanks to his pills. He gave the prescription to all of his contacts in the government, Admiralty and LMS, indeed all his correspondents, and sent a paper on it to the Epidemiological

Society of London. It had never failed, he said, but he had been shy about publicizing it before for fear that it sounded like a quack's miracle cure.

The Livingstones and Kirk welcomed the missionaries and the *Pioneer* to the Zambezi mouth in February 1861. They were led by Charles Frederick Mackenzie, who had been consecrated Anglican Bishop of Central Africa in Cape Town the previous month. He was an athlete, cricketer and Cambridge mathematician, and had been Archdeacon of Natal, where he quit a committee arranging the South African synod in protest at black churches not being given equal representation. He brought six men with him, lay and clergy, educated and artisan, and more were to follow.

The missionaries got on very well with the Zambezi trio. Mackenzie said Livingstone was "most kind and excellent", and "as for Kirk, we are the greatest possible cronies". Livingstone and Kirk agreed that the bishop was "the A1", "a trump of a fellow", always ready to roll up his sleeves and be useful. And yet they immediately had a major disagreement about their next steps. Mackenzie expected Livingstone to take his team straight up the Shire to Nyasa so that they could get on with their work. Livingstone planned a more exploratory route up the Rovuma, 800 miles up the coast. Mackenzie proposed to let Livingstone and his companions investigate the Rovuma on foot while the missionaries took the boat. Livingstone said he was very unhappy about them going alone through unfamiliar territory after what had happened to the Linyanti missionaries.

They debated, quite amicably, for days, but eventually Mackenzie capitulated. Dropping five of the missionaries off at a naval base on the Comoro Islands 200 miles off the coast for safekeeping, the rest of the party headed up the Rovuma in the *Pioneer*. It was a 400-mile journey, and they covered thirty before they realized that the water level was falling by six inches a day, and had to turn back in a hurry before they were stranded. This,

Livingstone explained in a letter to *The Times*, was a temporary
setback due entirely to the late delivery of the *Pioneer*. He added
that the changing water level and the muddiness of the water
suggested that the Rovuma did not come from Nyasa after all,
but possibly from Lake Tanganyika.

The team collected the other missionaries from the Comoros,
and while there they witnessed a further stage of the illicit
slave trade, which Livingstone also reported in his letter to *The
Times*. France, like Portugal, was a signatory to international
anti-slave trading treaties, but these allowed its existing slaves to
be transported from one island to another. So a French captain
bought sixty new slaves from the African coast for twenty-two
rix-dollars (about £1 13s) each, sailed them to Comoro, and
there bought forged papers certifying that the slaves were from
there, allowing him to transport them openly to other French
colonies. "The Emperor of France is said to have declared that
if the so called 'free emigration' were the slave trade he would
not have it at any price – here unfortunately his people have it
at the prices above stated."

The *Pioneer* headed up the Zambezi towards the Shire, covering
the eighty miles to Mazaro in sixteen hours, compared to the
ten days of their previous attempt. They took a little detour up
the Zambezi to Senna, to collect cotton processed on the gins
they had left there. Kirk reckoned it was better quality than US
cotton, and what they had bought for 8d would sell for 5s/10d.
They found an obscure design fault with the boat: when it did
come upon sandbanks, the engines filled with sand, demanding
a few days' repair work. On the Shire itself they had a painfully
slow journey, once getting stuck on a sandbank for a fortnight.
Everyone caught malaria and took Livingstone's pills.

In July 1861, they dropped off two missionaries, Henry
Rowley and Horace Waller, to start a mission station at Chibisa's.
The others, leaving the *Pioneer* there, proceeded past the rapids
on foot, with twenty-one porters, mostly Makololo. Mackenzie

wore a wide-brimmed wide-awake hat and a belt from which hung a large bag of seed and a can of oil, and he carried his bishop's crook in one hand and a gun in the other. "We were a strange party," he said.

The missionaries had been reluctant to carry guns at first, but Livingstone won them over to his policy of ballistic deterrent. Villagers would take every advantage of the defenceless, he argued, but respected a show of force, making guns "the greatest pacificators in the world if you have peaceful intentions yourself".

In fact, they heard in the villages they passed that the highlands they were going to had become a war zone. Representatives of the Manganja tribe came to meet them in Chibisa's and asked for their help against the Yao (or Ajawa), who were raiding their villages for slaves. The Yao had Portuguese guns, Rowley reports, and sold their prisoners to the Portuguese, who then sold them not to overseas plantations but to African chiefs inland in exchange for ivory. He added, from later discoveries, that they were taking 200 slaves a week from Nyasaland, and that they had had none before Livingstone forged the path.

This news raised a hard question for the missionaries about the use of violence. They had agreed they would resort to violence in self-defence, up to, but not including, killing; they would rather die than kill those they had come to save. But how about defending those they had come to save from one another? "I thought I should be guided to a right course," Mackenzie wrote to his supervisor, Bishop Samuel Wilberforce, the son of William, "if the emergency should occur, which did not seem very likely; and praying for such guidance, I went on without coming to a decision on the point."

On 16 July, while Bishop Mackenzie was away bathing, they heard that a large caravan of slaves was coming towards them en route to Tete. They discussed whether to intervene. If they freed the slaves, the Portuguese could retaliate by seizing the considerable property they had left in Tete, and they might make enemies of their prospective neighbours who depended on the slave trade. On the other hand, Livingstone urged, they were settling here precisely for the purpose of fighting the slave trade, and here it was right in front of them, "dogging us where previously they durst not venture, and, on pretence of being 'our children', setting one tribe against another". The settlers resolved to take an implacable stance from the start. "Logic is out of place", Livingstone said in retrospect, "when the question with a true hearted man is, whether his brother man is to be saved or not."

Within minutes, the train of slaves came round the hill into the valley. There were eighty-four of them, most of them naked. Most were women and children, roped together by the neck. The men were bound in pairs, with cleft sticks six inches thick and six feet long fastened round their necks with a metal bolt. The slaves were driven by black guards "jauntily" bearing muskets and blowing tin horns, Livingstone said. "They seemed to feel that they were doing a very noble thing, and might proudly march with an air of triumph." They recognized the leader as the slave of Major Sicard.

The settlers confronted the slavers, who ran away – apart from the leader, who was seized by the Makololo – leaving the slaves, their luggage and four guns. The slaves knelt and slowly clapped their hands in thanks. The settlers cut the ropes binding the women and children, and as the bishop, returning from his bath, had a saw among his tools they slowly cut the men free. As the slaves had been carrying food, they were told to cook it for themselves, making a fire from their broken yokes, and to clothe themselves from the calico they carried as currency.

The settlers heard the slaves' stories. Two women had been shot the previous day for trying to untie their ropes. An old man had collapsed in exhaustion and was killed with an axe. When a woman had insisted she could not carry a large bundle of hoes because of her month-old baby, the slavers took the baby off her hands and bashed its brains out. A small boy said to the Makololo, "The others tied and starved us, you cut the ropes and tell us to eat; what sort of people are you?" The British told them about their planned settlement and invited them to join it. Most agreed. (Rowley, who was in Chibisa's, says half of them came; Mackenzie and Livingstone say that all did; the final total suggests somewhere in between.) This gave the settlement a population, so everything seemed to be working out happily and neatly. Livingstone told them it had taken him a long time to win the trust of Tswana tribes, so they were lucky to have achieved the same result in moments.

They met three more slave caravans on the way, and did the same thing each time. "As we had begun," said Livingstone, "it was of no use to do things by halves." They freed a total of 148 slaves, of whom 117 stayed with them.

Bishop Mackenzie felt rather ambivalent about the aggressive way in which they were entering the pastures of their new flock. He entirely agreed with Livingstone's policy of liberation by force, or a show of it, but was definite that it was Livingstone's work and that the missionaries, as Christian pastors, were merely supporting him in it.

News of what the British were doing spread. A trading party with a hundred slaves changed their route to avoid them, so Kirk and four Makololo chased them. They got as far as Chibisa's without catching up, and there Kirk told Rowley about the liberations. Rowley, delighted at this "happy inauguration of our mission work", told Kirk that that same day, a squadron from Tete had passed the village, a hundred armed slaves led by a Portuguese officer. Rowley had asked the "Chibisians" what was happening, and was told that they were going to take slaves from the Manganja and "claimed us [the missionaries] for brothers." He had decided he did not have the authority or power for prior restraint, but asked the villagers to keep a watch out for their return. Now he and Kirk decided to follow them up the river towards the cataracts, Kirk and the Makololo on foot, Rowley in the boat.

"Had the boat done as much as it might have done," says Rowley, "we should have cut them off, but to our chagrin we learnt that they passed over the river just above where the boat halted. Vexation at this failure gave me fever. I was ill for several days."

Later that month, however, Rowley received much more cheerful news. The slaving party had returned past Chibisa's empty-handed. The leader sent a message to the British there saying that he had heard what Livingstone was doing, had taken no slaves, and had no quarrel with the British.

The bishop's party decided to establish the mission at Magomero, which belonged to the Manganja who had appealed to them for protection from the Yao, between the river and Lake Shirwa. Bishop Mackenzie had been considering the Mount Soche region, which was much closer to the river, more fertile and more attractive; but, according to Waller, Livingstone persuaded the bishop to stay, saying, "If you fall back to Mount Soche, all this densely populated country will go before the Ajawas; if you take your stand here it will be saved." Mackenzie writes of it as his own choice, but either way he had decided to ask Chigunda, the last remaining Manganja chief in the area, to let them stay with him, when Chigunda spontaneously asked them to do so.

Two days later, on 22 July, they heard that Yao raiders were on their way, and now attacking a Manganja village a few miles away. Livingstone and his companions, followed by Chigunda's men, went out to meet them. Refugees streamed past them, and they saw the smoke of three burning villages. Before entering the battlefield, they knelt and the bishop led them in prayer, while in the distance they heard a mixture of war cries and wailing. They then stood to see some sixty or seventy

Yao soldiers approaching with their slaves. The Yao headman climbed on an ant-hill to size up this assortment of British men, Makololo and Manganja.

There was nothing necessarily disastrous about the situation. Livingstone had repeatedly faced down armed aggressors, with a display either of arms or of unarmed nerve, without letting anyone get hurt on either side. The missionaries certainly did not want to shed blood, and the Manganja – in theory – wanted their attackers to leave them alone, while the Yao did not have the weapons to compete with British rifles.

But, as Livingstone started walking towards the Yao, assuring them he only wanted to talk, the Manganja behind him were carried away by their moment of strength and let out war cries and aggressive taunts. The Yao immediately fell into assault positions around them, concealed in long grass a hundred yards away, while their slaves ran for freedom. A large number of reinforcements ran to join the Yao from the village. Livingstone again called that they came in peace, but the Yao started closing in, performing their war dance and firing poisoned arrows, one landing either side of Livingstone, one catching a Manganja on the arm. The British returned fire, the bishop insisting that Livingstone use his gun instead of him. Six Yao were killed and their comrades, quickly realizing they could not withstand such guns, retreated, shouting that they would follow them and kill them where they slept. Livingstone burned the village to spoil their spoils.

Finding themselves led onto this unexpectedly military path, the British discussed how far to follow it. Bishop Mackenzie wanted to pursue all the Yao, free their slaves and drive them out of the region, but Livingstone persuaded them to wait and see what effect this skirmish would have on the slavers before engaging them again.

In August 1861, Livingstone went to Lake Nyasa to explore it fully, investigating the suitability of the land for trade and colonization, and whether it was the source of Rovuma. He took with him Charles, Kirk and twenty Makololo, and a four-oared boat they collected from the *Pioneer*. En route, they saw a party of slave traders from Chibisa's, from which Kirk concluded: "The whole country is deeply engaged in the slave trade.... While the Portuguese remain sole possessors of the Zambezi, the labour of stopping the slave trade will be great."

They got the boat past the Murchison Cataracts and onto the lake on 2 September. One night before they sailed, they were robbed of everything they had apart from the clothes they slept in and cloth and bags used as pillows, which fortunately contained their guns and ammunition. Charles wanted to turn back, but David said they could make new clothes. He had planned to leave the Makololo there, but it was clearly unsafe, so they followed them along the shore on foot and the boat had to keep to their pace.

The shores seemed too swampy for colonization, but they were densely populated. This should have been good news for trade and provisions, but the people were being raided by the Matabele – the Zulus who had previously terrorized the Tswana in South Africa. Their gardens were destroyed and their villages descended into anarchic violence. The Makololo were repeatedly threatened. The sailors saw skulls in the trees and bones in the reeds. They heard stories of Matabele attacks from survivors: "They select a few of the strongest young men and women," Kirk reports, "and carry them off. All others they murder that the young may have nowhere to flee to and also to satisfy their desire for blood. As an Englishman loves to kill game, so they kill men for sport."

For Kirk and Charles, the journey was their worst ordeal of heat and hunger yet, with nothing to do but sail in the sun and sleep amid marshes. "The inactivity," recalled Kirk, "and pains in the bones and joints from the sun, the gradual emaciation, the fevers and the starvation of that Nyasa journey combine to make it the hardest, most trying, and most disagreeable of all our journeys. It is the only one I have no pleasure in looking back on." He added that David did not seem to mind in the least.

The Makololo complained that the journey was pointlessly dangerous, and reminded Livingstone that he had promised to send some of them back that year. On 3 October they went on strike, so Livingstone agreed to walk with them. On the first day he was with them they lost contact with the boat and it took Kirk four days to track them down, upon which Livingstone's first words to his unimpressed rescuer were: "What on earth made you run away and leave us?"

Meeting a troop of seven Matabele, Livingstone approached them unarmed. They banged their shields and demanded goat, but when he said he had nothing left to give them they left them alone.

They were running out of food and time to get back. One night both of Charles's bags were stolen as he slept on them. Kirk and Charles met Arab traders in ivory and slaves on a dhow, who told them the Rovuma did not flow from the lake, but they were on the wrong side to confirm that for themselves.

They turned back, having failed to reach the end of the lake and complete their survey. The Makololo quarrelled with Livingstone and quit the expedition to go elephant hunting. He had found nowhere suitable for colonization or trade. He had failed to consolidate the one significant achievement of the Zambezi expedition, gaining access to Nyasaland, by connecting Magomero with supplies of local produce. Kirk had once again finally had enough: "My own mind is now fully made up to be off by the very first opportunity."

Chapter 19

DEFEAT

Returning from Nyasa in November, the explorers found the missionaries at Chibisa's, and heard two pieces of news. First, Mackenzie had been persuaded by the Manganja to attack two Yao camps to rescue captives, though the second was empty, so he just burned it; Livingstone and Kirk offered "friendly disapproval" of this more aggressive approach. Secondly, a new missionary from Oxford, Henry de Wint Burrup, arrived, telling them two ships were on their way up from Cape Town carrying missionary reinforcements, including Mary Livingstone, Mackenzie's elder sister Anne, the Scottish colonialist James Stewart, and James Rae, who brought the steamer which Livingstone had commissioned, the *Lady Nyassa*, as well as Burrup's wife.

Livingstone took the *Pioneer* to meet them at the Zambezi delta. Mackenzie wanted to come too, but Livingstone considered it a dereliction of duty so soon after having made enemies of the Yao, demonstrating emotional over-reliance on his sister. As a compromise they agreed that Mackenzie would come to meet them at a junction of the Shire fifty miles from the Magomero mission.

Livingstone set off from Chibisa's on 15 November, and within three days the *Pioneer* was stuck on a sandbank, where it stayed for five weeks. In that time the carpenter Robert Fayers became the first European to die from malaria under Livingstone's care. Livingstone was so late that on the day he was supposed to meet Mackenzie on the way back from the delta, he was passing the meeting point still on his way down. Mackenzie was not there though, so Livingstone proceeded south without him.

Mary Livingstone's ship, the *Gorgon*, reached the Zambezi to find no sign of David, and so put to sea again for three weeks, in which time it was nearly destroyed by a tornado. After their latest separation four years ago, Mary had given birth to a daughter, Anna Mary, in Kuruman in November 1858, and taken her back to Scotland to rejoin her other children. There she had again had an utterly miserable time, suffering depression and spiritual crises and drinking heavily. Dr Stewart, who sailed with them, had taught her son Thomas and was a good friend to her. He took great pains to ensure that no one but him witnessed her nightly drunkenness, and succeeded, at the cost of convincing their fellow travellers that they were having an affair.

Once reunited on 31 January 1862, Mary and David were stuck in the lower reaches of the Zambezi for months. To Livingstone's annoyance, the *Lady Nyassa*, which he had instructed should be brought out whole, came in twenty-four pieces, to be carried upstream and built at Shupanga. There were also ninety newcomers with a great deal of luggage for him to ferry resentfully through the malarial waters, and the *Pioneer* was repeatedly grounded, struggling almost as badly as the *Ma-Robert*. More than one member of the party thought Livingstone made things worse by his disorganization – "constant vacillations, blunders, delays, and want of common thought and foresight", in the words of a sailor.

The missionaries offered to take Mary with them when they went north to healthier territory, leaving David to assemble his new steamboat, but she refused. David wrote to her brother in February, mentioning this and saying that "if she gets fever, up she must go, though it be ever so much against the grain". Mary added between the lines, "Do not believe him."

That month, Kirk and the captain of the *Gorgon* took Anne Mackenzie to meet her brother and Mrs Burrup her husband. Still not finding the bishop at the river junction, they continued to Chibisa's, where on 4 March they heard what had happened. The bishop's party had failed to meet Livingstone at the agreed date because they were attacked en route. Some of Mackenzie's African crew were kidnapped, so he led a counter-attack in which one of his men was killed. He retreated to Magomero, and returned immediately with Burrup and three Makololo in a canoe. They travelled in torrential rain, and lost their food and medicine when the boat capsized. They arrived at the river junction feverish and famished, three days too late to catch Livingstone. They sheltered there for twenty days, before Mackenzie died of malaria. The others returned to Magomero, where Burrup died of the same disease within days.

Kirk marked Mackenzie's grave with a bamboo cross, and Livingstone later erected a stone cross nearby. The women returned to the *Pioneer*, so feverish they had to be carried on board. When Livingstone heard their news he put his head in his hand and said, "This will hurt us all." In his journal he added, "I will not swerve a hair's breadth from my work while life is spared." The women returned to Britain.

While the ferrying continued, in the evenings David and Mary caught up with each other, taking riverside walks, and, in David's words, "more than would be thought by some a decorous amount of merriment and play". Then on 21 April Mary suddenly fell seriously ill. She was taken indoors at Shupanga and David stayed at her bedside for six days. "My dearie, my dearie," he wept, raising his voice as she was half-deaf from quinine, "you are going to leave me. Are you resting on Jesus?" On the sixth day she became unconscious and David called for Stewart to commit her soul to the Lord. Stewart found him in tears. The two of them, with Kirk, knelt in prayer and Mary died an hour later. They buried her under a baobab tree.

David wrote in his journal,

> *I am left alone in the world by one whom I felt to be a part of myself. I hope it may, by divine grace, lead me to realise heaven as my home, and that she has but preceded me in the journey.*
>
> *Oh my Mary, my Mary! How often we have longed for a quiet home, since you and I were cast*

adrift at Kolobeng; surely the removal by a kind
Father who knoweth our frame means that He
rewarded you by taking you to the best home, the
eternal one in the heavens.[18]

David was buckled by his loss. He quickly returned to work, but
was more self-absorbed than ever, his moods dark and volatile.
He wrote to his mother, "This unlooked for bereavement quite
crushes and takes the heart out of me. Everything else that
happened in my career only made the mind rise to overcome it,
but this takes away all my strength."

It took two months to build the *Lady Nyassa* at Shupanga.
Another old companion rejoined them there: Richard Thornton
returned from Kilimanjaro and started geological work for
Livingstone again.

Meanwhile the missionaries at Magomero faced continual
conflict with the Yao, and on 6 May quit the settlement to live
at Chibisa's. In fact Chibisa had been driven from the village
by the Yao, and his people were now ruled by the Makololo
who had quit Livingstone's Nyasa trip to go elephant hunting.
The Makololo also took control of the other Manganja tribes of
the region, successfully led them against the Yao, and attacked
slaving expeditions, releasing all but the most desirable captives
to live with the British.

James Stewart, having been drawn here by Livingstone's
glowing descriptions of a region begging to be colonized,
had been increasingly dismayed by the war-torn and famished
sights along the Shire, and now decided he had been seriously
deceived. "His accursed lies," he wrote, "have caused much
toil, trouble, anxiety and loss of life, as well as money and
reputation, and I have been led a dance over half the world to
accomplish nothing."

With even Kirk ready to leave and government sponsorship
likely to be withdrawn before long, Livingstone knew that his
expedition was reaching an end, but he wanted to make one

more attempt to accomplish something by taking boats up the Rovuma, mapping it, locating its source and perhaps even finding a route to the lake. He took Kirk, his brother, Rae, and his African crew in the *Pioneer*, and they went via the Comoro Islands to buy supplies for the missionaries.

During the sea journey, Kirk found Livingstone moodier than ever, and learned to give him a particularly wide berth if he started humming "The Happy Land". A warship towed them from the Comoros to Rovuma, arriving on 9 September 1862, lent Livingstone two sailors for the river trip and took Rae back when, to Livingstone's disgust, he pleaded illness.

They found the river mouth shallower than ever and Kirk thought it was obviously unnavigable, but Livingstone insisted on proceeding. They left the *Pioneer* and wound their way through tortuous shoals in two small boats, constantly having to drag them across sand. Kirk argued that if the Africans deserted them they could be stuck for three months; Livingstone replied that "if he risked nothing he would gain nothing". Kirk wrote in his journal:

> *The infatuation which blinds him, I cannot comprehend, getting the boats jammed up in a river where they cannot float and where it will be impossible to return. It seems madness and to follow a man running such risks for the empty glory of geographical discovery is more than I would consent to... I can come to no other conclusion than that Dr. L. is out of his mind.* [19]

On 19 September, they were ambushed and surrounded by a tribe armed with guns and poisoned arrows. Livingstone explained their peaceful intentions, and eventually they were allowed to pass after paying a toll. But then the villagers opened fire after all, leaving four bullet holes in the sail of Livingstone's boat. The British returned fire and Kirk and one of the crew each killed a man.

They continued for another week, Kirk angry that Livingstone cared more for discovery than whether they lived to report it to anyone. On 27 September, 114 miles from the mouth, Livingstone concluded that the river could not flow from Nyasa and was not navigable, and turned back.

It remained to get the supplies up the Shire to the mission station and the *Lady Nyassa* to the lake she was named for. The mission had been the one practical result of the Zambezi expedition, but if Livingstone could find a way for a steamship to get from the sea to the great lake, he could conclude the expedition with a second. The boat, its engines not yet fitted, was towed by the *Pioneer*, then, after a nasty crash, tied to its side. They were grounded for three weeks between January and February 1863.

Kirk started to find Livingstone not just a manageable eccentric, but intolerable. The flashpoint was a mountain expedition which Kirk wanted to lead for the sake of his botanical studies and for the health of himself and others who were suffering from malaria. Livingstone had agreed, but, when it came to it, he only allowed them one day for it. Kirk was furious for days, complaining in his journal about "his narrow selfish mind": "Dr Livingstone's word of honour will not have much value in my mind again... I have been grossly ill used." Livingstone's only motives, he believed, were the desire to collect his own belongings as fast and cheaply as possible and "some low sort of revenge" for Kirk's diminished opinion of him since the Rovuma trip.

Perhaps Kirk's tolerance was finally overcome by what he described now as "the fever which hangs to us, like poison in the system, destroying all activity and contentment", but finally wrecking even his friendship sounds like the crowning achievement of Livingstone's extraordinary succession of broken relationships. In fact it turns out to be the one Livingstone bothered to mend, apparently because he had no idea it was broken.

Rae shut himself in the *Lady Nyassa* wanting nothing to do
with anyone. Stewart, finding every new aspect of the promised
land he had come to colonize worse than the last, merely
wanted nothing to do with Livingstone. He quit the expedition
and on 1 February "went down the river bank a short way and
threw with all my strength into the turbid muddy weed-covered
Zambesi my copy of certain *Missionary Travels in South Africa*".

The Shire, which had so impressed them with its fertility
and potential three years before, was now a sickening scene,
devastated by war and drought, Makololo and Yao, and above
all the Portuguese slave trade. Kirk reckoned the Manganja tribe
were almost extinct. Livingstone reported:

> *Dead bodies floated past us daily, and in the*
> *mornings the paddles had to be cleared of corpses*
> *caught by the floats during the night. For scores of*
> *miles the entire population of the valley was swept*
> *away by this savage Mariano, who is again as he was*
> *before the great Portuguese slave agent. It made the*
> *heart ache to see the widespread desolation; the river-*
> *banks once so populous, all silent; the villages burned*
> *down, and an oppressive stillness reigning where*
> *formerly crowds of eager sellers appeared with the*
> *various products of their industry … The sight and*
> *smell of dead bodies was every where. Many skeletons*
> *lay beside the path, where in their weakness they had*
> *fallen and expired. Ghastly living forms of girls and*
> *boys, with dull dead eyes, were crouching beside some*
> *of the huts. A few more miserable days of their terrible*
> *hunger, and they would be with the dead.* [20]

The above passage is from Livingstone's *Narrative*, written,
he said afterwards, with "most distressing caution" to avoid
accusations of exaggeration. He could not bear to write or think
of those "hell scenes" and years later he would suddenly wake

up in the night reliving the experience, and have to get up and walk about. Philosophers doubt if there is a hell, he said, "but I have been in it".

They met the missionaries and heard that one more had died. Another died while they were there. Rowley reckoned Livingstone's expedition was at its lowest ebb: "Fever has laid hold of all the European crew, the officers are all but in rebellion, and the Dr. daily becomes more incapable of self-control." On 19 March, Livingstone celebrated his fiftieth birthday.

In April they reached the Murchison Cataracts, and Livingstone directed the building of a road to carry the *Lady Nyassa* round them. While working on that they heard that Thornton had died of a combination of malaria and dysentery after walking to Tete and back to bring food for the mission station. Days later Charles announced he was finally leaving the expedition. Livingstone told Kirk he might as well go too, but arranged the parting in a way Kirk considered sneaky, grasping and more concerned for his own convenience than Kirk's safety. Before they were able to leave, Livingstone was debilitated with dysentery for a month. Kirk and Charles stayed with him until he had recovered, then left on 19 May.

Kirk's confidence in Livingstone had never recovered since the Rovuma trip. He largely kept his feelings to himself out of a sense of propriety, and the belief that, if they argued, Livingstone's vindictive streak would lay waste everything he had done over the last four years. Livingstone himself had been increasingly taciturn. And so their collaboration ended in a silence which Livingstone read as mutual understated admiration and which Kirk read as mutual sullen animosity.

Livingstone and Rae remained, making the Murchison bypass, and taking apart the *Lady Nyassa* to be carried on it. At one point, Livingstone went off to collect the little boat he had used on his last visit to the lake, only to find it had been destroyed in a forest fire.

They were racing against time, and on 3 July 1863, Livingstone received a despatch from the Foreign Secretary recalling the expedition. While commending Livingstone's zeal, Lord Russell said that as he had failed to find a route into Africa through the Zambezi or the Rovuma, the purpose of the expedition was finished; it was hoped they would finish immediately, or Livingstone could have longer to draw things to a close, but salaries would not be paid past the end of the year. The *Lady Nyassa* was never going to reach the lake. Rae started reassembling it to return with the *Pioneer*. It had never even had its engines working.

The despatch was brought to Livingstone by Mackenzie's replacement as Bishop of Nyasaland, William Tozer. Tozer announced that he was withdrawing the mission to Mount Morambula near the mouth of the Shire for the sake of health and safety. This meant leaving all the slaves Mackenzie had rescued – an act Tozer considered highway robbery – apart from the orphan boys. Livingstone was unimpressed, and another missionary, Waller, quit the mission in anger. To save them from recapture, Waller arranged to take them to Cape Town, with Livingstone's help. Then Henry Rowley was sent home for the sake of his health, leaving only the agriculturalist Arthur Adams of the original mission team.

As for Livingstone's return, the Shire waters were too shallow to sail for some months, so he seized the day and went on one last march, exploring the land west of Lake Nyasa, taking a band of Makololo, Yao, Manganja, and the sailor Thomas Ward.

Livingstone made no great geographical discoveries on this expedition; his main finding was that slave raiding went further than he did. He saw countless refugees who looked like "human skeletons swathed in brown and wrinkled leather", leaving him with "an overpowering sense of helplessness to alleviate human woe". Returning to the *Lady Nyassa* on 1 November, Livingstone was frustrated to have to wait two more months for the rains that allowed the ship to sail. "We might have visited Lake Bemba," he protested.

Considerably more depressing was the news that Bishop Tozer's retreat had gone as far as leaving the mainland for Zanzibar. Livingstone wrote to him imploring him to stay, and saying, "… if you go, the last ray of hope for this wretched downtrodden people disappears." To a friend in the Cape, he wrote, "This I believe to be the first instance in modern times in which missionaries have voluntarily turned tail… He is a grievous disappointment to me and much more so than our own recall… I feel as if I could sit down and cry rather than write."

Livingstone collected Waller and his abandoned ex-slaves and carried them down to the Zambezi delta. There Livingstone returned the *Pioneer* to the navy and headed off alone in the *Lady Nyassa*.

The first time Livingstone left Africa, though he could not have imagined the acclaim that awaited him at home, he left in the knowledge that he had made a unique achievement in his coast-to-coast hike, and in the belief that he had opened a trade route into the heart of southern Africa, and in the hope that the commercial development that followed would bring with it social development, Christian mission and a check to the reawakening slave trade.

This time, despite the support of the government to the tune now of £30,000, and help from the navy and numerous assistants, he had failed, failed and failed again to open waterways into the region. No trade or industry had been established, the mission had fled the field, and the slave trade was burgeoning, more healthily than if Livingstone had never come. For all his mountainous self-belief, Livingstone could not entirely escape the knowledge that his great work had failed.

There was one meagre consolation: for the first time in his life, Livingstone was his own master and could go wherever in the world he chose. He went to Bombay.

Chapter 20

FURLOUGH

Livingstone was unemployed, and having put the money he earned from his book in trust for his family, he owed almost three-quarters of it to pay for the *Lady Nyassa*, so his first priority was to sell the ship. He was offered a good price by the Portuguese at Tete, but knew that they would use it in the slave trade, so he refused their offer. He took it to Zanzibar in April 1864, and there failed to get a decent offer, so he decided to leave it in Bombay for now, getting a fast passage home to discuss the matter with the man to whom he owed £6,000 for the boat, his university friend James Young.

Livingstone sailed the river vessel across the Indian Ocean. He had planned to take Rae as engineer, but Rae refused, so he did it without, taking a British sailor, stoker and carpenter, and a crew of nine African men and boys. One of the boys was Chuma, a Yao slave who had been freed by the British in July 1861; another was Susi, who was from Shupanga, had worked for Sicard and then became one of Livingstone's wood cutters. They would both be Livingstone's helpers for the rest of his life.

Livingstone had a month to get to India to be sure of beating the monsoon, and reckoned they could do it in eighteen days. They had enough coal for three-and-a-half days of continuous steaming, so much of that time they would be depending on the wind. And the sailor said there was something wrong with the engine, but he could not tell what.

The journey in fact took six weeks, thanks to poor winds. Livingstone had time to write about his ideas for British involvement in Africa, which he continued to explore as ever: there should be no colony "as the term colony is usually understood", he wrote in his journal, but by the management of agriculture, trade and all public matters "the Englishman would be an unmixed advantage to everyone below and around him, for he would fill a place which is now practically vacant".

Luckily, the monsoon held off longer than expected, but they were still 165 miles from Bombay when the weather started to worsen. They survived three days of furious squalls before reaching the harbour on 13 June 1864.

Livingstone stayed just eleven days in India, but it was long enough to become friends with Sir Bartle Frere, the British governor, exchanging intelligence and strategies on the slave trade. He left the *Lady Nyassa* in the care of a British officer and returned to England. He spent a week in London, and though he had a rather more subdued welcome than before, he was entertained warmly by the Murchisons, and by the Palmerstons at Downing Street. In August he went to Scotland to talk to Young, who cheerfully wrote off Livingstone's £6,000 debt, and kept the money coming. Livingstone then went on to Hamilton to see his family. Four of his five children lived with his mother and sisters there.

The eldest, Robert, who was eighteen, was not there but, David now discovered, was fighting in the American Civil War. He had disappointed his father, and the trustees who had oversight of him, by taking no interest in education and refusing to go to college. He wanted to join the navy, but the trustees refused – though David would have approved. After Mary died, David summoned Robert to join him in Nyasaland, so he went to South Africa in June 1863. He made his haphazard way north, stayed with the Moffats' widowed daughter-in-law in Natal and borrowed a pound from her, but failed to make contact with his father and turned back to Cape Town. There he took a job on a ship bound for Boston, and on his arrival joined the Unionist army. It has often been said that Robert joined the fight against US slavery to redeem and prove himself in his father's eyes after

a misspent youth, but both the tone and details of the letter that
David received from him in October make that seem unlikely:

> *My dear Sir,*
>   *Hearing that you have returned to England I
> undertake to address a few lines to you, not with any
> hope that you will be interested in me but simply to
> explain the position...*
>   *Your agent Mr. Rutherford advised me to find
> employment on board a brig which brought me to
> Boston, America. Here I was kidnapped and one
> morning, after going to bed on board ship, I found
> myself enlisted in the U.S. army.*
>   *I have been in one battle and two skirmishes, and
> expect to be in another terrific battle before long.
> God in His mercy has spared me as yet. I have never
> hurt anyone knowingly in battle, have always fired
> high, and in that furious madness which accompanies
> a bayonet charge and which seems to possess every
> soldier I controlled my passion and took the man who
> surrendered prisoner.*
>   *The rebels are not likely to hold out much longer
> as we have nearly all their railroads. My craving
> for travelling is not yet satisfied, though if I had the
> chance that I threw away of being educated, I should
> think myself only too much blessed. I have changed
> my name, for I am convinced that to bear your name
> here would lead to further dishonour to it.*
>   *I am at present in this hospital, exposure and
> fatigue having given me ague fever.*
>   *Your quondam son, Robert.* [21]

As for the rest of the family, David's mother did not at first
recognize him, while David in turn did not recognize his son

Thomas, a sickly fifteen-year-old he had last seen aged nine. Agnes was seventeen, Oswell thirteen, and Anna Mary, whom he now saw for the first time, five. She was shy of him and found him rather shy of her. He gave her a black doll which she did not think much of, and a kiss which tickled, and all in all she enjoyed his company rather less than Charles's. "My father was absorbed in work," she recollected late in life, "and I can only remember him as always writing letters."

Livingstone had been suffering from severe bleeding piles, was urged to undergo surgery, and arranged an operation in Glasgow, but then cancelled it, telling Kirk he did not "like to get my infirmities put into the newspapers". Considering how it affected his final expedition, it seems a sad and fateful decision. Then again, one can hardly lament Livingstone's treatment by fate, as realistically he should have been dead a dozen times over already.

In September, David went with his daughter Agnes to Bath to give a lecture – "after many a cold *shiver* in the mere prospect of it", he said. He used it to report and denounce Portuguese slave trading in and around Mozambique. The speech caused enough of a stir to provoke an official response from Lisbon, accusing him of "exploring for no other purpose than to drive the Portuguese out of Africa". This encouraged him to expand the lecture into a book, which by the time it was finished had become a full-length account of the Zambezi expedition, *Narrative of an Expedition to the Zambesi*. He wrote it while staying with Agnes in Newstead Abbey near Nottingham, the stately home at one time of Lord Byron and now of William Webb, a big game hunter Livingstone knew from Kolobeng. Alice Webb, William's daughter, recalled in later life, like many others, that Livingstone spoke English like a second language; more specially, she described how Agnes and David grew from "natural companion[s]" to close friends. They were both, she said, simple, direct, laconic, dutiful and courageous, and "The pride both the two took in each other was touching to witness." Towards the end of this period, Livingstone wrote to Murray, his publisher: "I ought to have been off ere now – though I have every comfort that I can desire here, I often take a sore longing to be in Africa. My family is my only chain."

Kirk and Stewart, both back in Britain, continued to discuss the subject of Livingstone in outraged terms. Kirk believed, wrongly, that Livingstone had secretly given the Foreign Office a bad report of Kirk's contribution to the Zambezi expedition, and told Stewart, "He is about as ungrateful and slippery a mortal as I ever came into contact with." Kirk was evidently so ready for Livingstone's vindictiveness when he finally turned against him that it took him a long time to realize that, as far as Livingstone was concerned, their friendship continued as happily as ever. Livingstone named a mountain range where the Shire leaves Lake Nyasa "Kirk's Range" in his book. He arranged with the government and Kew Gardens a £1,200 commission for Kirk, "a capital fellow", to write up his botanical discoveries. Kirk refused, until Livingstone finally persuaded him, likening the work to Darwin's *Voyage of the Beagle*. He even hoped that Kirk would be his only companion on his next African expedition. Eventually Kirk was persuaded that Livingstone was genuine and came to help him in his writing at Newstead Abbey, though he had no intention of joining another expedition.

Livingstone's plan for his next venture was to return to Nyasaland via the Rovuma, and then head west or north-west into the unknown. In January 1865, Murchison wrote suggesting a "purely geographical" expedition, following the route Livingstone already had in mind, to discover the watersheds of South Africa and the sources of the Nile. He added that if Livingstone preferred to spend the rest of his life "on the mud and sandbanks of England" or to return to his political and religious concerns in Africa, he would ask Kirk instead.

The proposal, and Livingstone's answer to it, offer an intriguing and invaluable insight into Livingstone's mind, his motivations and priorities. Were Christian mission and the suppression of the slave trade real passions for him or mere excuses for exploration? Here he was offered the opportunity to indulge in pure exploration, with no other duties. His response, however, was not entirely straightforward.

According to his journal, he told Murchison, "I could only feel in the way of duty by working as a missionary." Two weeks later he told Young even more emphatically, "I would not consent to go simply as a geographer, but as a missionary, and do geography by the way, because I feel I am in the way of duty when trying either to enlighten these poor people, or open their land to lawful commerce."

This seems a clear refusal, but his actual letter to Murchison, or the part that survives, was rather less clear:

> *I should like the exploration you propose very much, and had already made up my mind to go... What my inclination leads me to prefer is to have intercourse with the people, and do what I can by talking, to enlighten them on the slave-trade, and give them some idea of our religion. It may not be much that I can do, but I feel when doing that I am not living in vain....*
>
> *To be debarred from spending most of my time in travelling, in exploration, and continual intercourse with the natives, I always felt to be a severe privation, and if I can get a few hearty native companions, I shall enjoy myself, and feel that I am doing my duty. As soon as my book is out, I shall start.* [22]

In the preface to his book, Livingstone said that the forthcoming expedition was proposed and aided by the Royal Geographical Society, but described the work as principally to establish "lawful trade and Christian Missions" for the moral and material benefit of Africans, adding the search for the watershed as if it were a sideline.

So on the one hand it seems Livingstone was not prepared to commit to a purely geographical expedition, and insisted on combining three vocations; on the other, he was prepared to give different readers different impressions of the balance between the three. His real priorities were only to be revealed in his actions.

The Foreign Office, having given Livingstone £5,000 and a consulate for his last expedition, offered him a commission "giving him authority over the chiefs from the Portuguese boundary to Abyssinia and Egypt", and no payment at all. Livingstone replied that the most insignificant government servant received pay and he would not "be treated like a charwoman". Eventually, the government gave him £500, as did the Royal Geographical Society, while James Young personally gave him £1,000. In February, Palmerston asked whether there was "anything that he could do for him". Livingstone asked for a treaty with Portugal granting access to Nyasaland via the Zambezi. It was not forthcoming, and Livingstone kicked himself when he realized it was an invitation to request the Order of the Bath.

In March he received news from Africa that upset him deeply. Sekeletu had died, and a Makololo civil war ensued, followed by an uprising of their subject tribes, at which the Makololo men fled and dispersed, leaving the women and children to the victors. "There is now," Livingstone concluded, "no Makololo tribe." His unhappiness cannot have been helped by the thought that if the British settlement for mission and trade which he had envisioned, indeed promised, had come about, this extinction would not have happened.

Livingstone completed his book in April. He gave co-author credit to Charles, because he had used his journal as a source. He also drew on Rae, Stewart, Waller and Kirk for information, while Oswell, with whom he exchanged weekly letters throughout his stay, proofread, and Agnes and Alice helped write out the final version. The book was a very pale sequel to *Missionary Travels*, a judgment reflected in its relatively poor sales. In part this was a natural result of the different events they recount: one, an ultimately triumphant trek across uncharted and dangerous territory, ending with a future full of challenge and promise; the other, a long series of abortive forays up three rivers, eventually fizzling out. But on top of that, when seen alongside the records of those involved, it is an epic of omission, Livingstone at his most inauthentic, and therefore unengaging.

It met with mixed reviews. The *Anthropological Review* said it was "not... a very interesting book", and the product of "poor naked mind". The *Fortnightly Review* summed up Livingstone's achievements thus:

> *Beginning with the announcement that the great Zambezi might be navigated in large vessels to the middle of the continent... Dr Livingstone was after a little time obliged to finish with the discovery, for so he called it, that flat bottomed boats can ascend to Tete. Thus a great national effort with unusual agitation ends in discovering what had been known to all the world for three centuries.* [23]

Alternatively, the *Quarterly Review* argued that "the discovery of the great Lake Nyasa would alone place Dr Livingstone high in the rank of African explorers".

Despite all this, however, it was a successful book in one important respect: it revealed the extent and bloodiness of the east African slave trade in a way that was taken seriously in high places.

In June, Livingstone heard of two deaths in the family. The first was Robert's – he had died of wounds in South Carolina.

David spoke of his loss as a sacrifice in the cause of anti-slavery: "I have lost my part in that gigantic struggle which the Highest guided to a consummation never contemplated by the southerners when they began." Seventeen days later, he heard that his mother had died and he went home for the funeral.

In August he took Agnes to London Zoo with Kirk and William Webb, and then left her in the care of Oswell, who told her, "If you are within a hundred miles of me let me know, and I will come and shake you by the hand. I will always come even to the end of the earth, if I can be of any use to you, or you want me." David then took Agnes to her new school in Paris, and made his way back to Bombay.

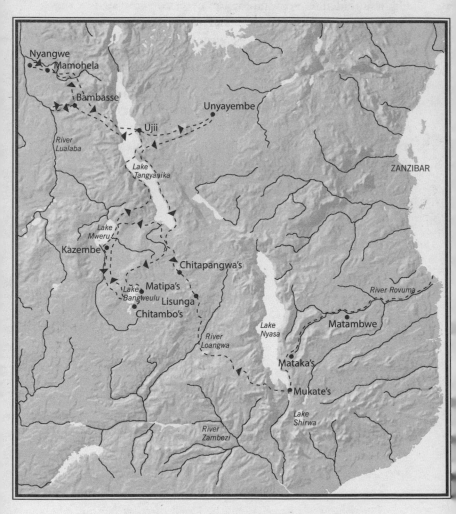

LAST JOURNEYS
1866-1873

Nyangwe
Mamohela
Bambasse
Unyayembe
Ujii
River Lualaba
Lake Tangyanika
ZANZIBAR
Lake Mweru
Kazembe
Chitapangwa's
Lake Bangweulu
Matipa's
Lisunga
Chitambo's
River Loangwa
Lake Nyasa
Matambwe
River Rovuma
Mataka's
Mukate's
Lake Shirwa
River Zambezi

Chapter 21

THE LAST
EXPEDITION

Arriving in Bombay on 11 September 1865, Livingstone set about selling the *Lady Nyassa*, eventually settling for just £2,300. While there, the posts of Consul and Agency-Surgeon at Zanzibar fell vacant. They were appointments of the governor, Bartle Frere, and Livingstone tried to get both of them for Kirk. Asked for a reference Livingstone told the governor that he knew of "no defect of character or temper". He failed with the former appointment, but Kirk was offered the latter. Despite having been offered a senior post at Kew and being engaged, he took up the post in January 1866, and married in 1867. Livingstone also got from Frere an assurance that he would help fight the slave trade.

Livingstone visited Zanzibar en route to the African mainland, and met the ruler of the island, Sultan Majid bin Said, who gave him an invaluable letter commanding the Arabs on the mainland, his subjects, to help him. While there Livingstone inspected Tozer's mission. The judgment he sent back to Waller in London was dismissive: "Tozer is trying the effect of gaudy dresses, banners and crosses as mission agencies." To Sedgwick, he was positively damning: "our mission there is virtually gagged… It is almost enough to make Mackenzie turn round in his grave to find his mission degraded to a mere chaplaincy to a consulate."

Livingstone was disgusted by the smell of the town, which he named "Stinkibar". The beach was used as a dump, making the air so fetid, he said, "one might cut out a slice and manure a

garden with it". The cholera epidemic which killed one in six of
the population in 1869–70 justified his disgust.

He visited a Zanzibari market where 300 slaves were on sale,
the majority, he reckoned, from Nyasa and the Shire valley. "The
teeth are examined, the cloth lifted to examine the lower limbs,
and a stick is thrown for the slave to bring, and thus exhibit his
paces. Some are dragged through the crowd by the hand, and
the price called out incessantly: most of the purchasers were
Northern Arabs and Persians."

Livingstone arrived on the mainland on 24 March 1866, and
recruited twenty-four porters to complete his crew. He already
had thirteen Indian soldiers (twelve sepoys led by a havildar)
provided by Frere, eight young men from the CMS school
for liberated slaves at Nasik, ten men from Johanna in the
Comoro Islands, plus four young men who had sailed with him
to Bombay in the *Lady Nyassa* and stayed there: Chuma and
another of Mackenzie's flock, Wakatiki; plus Susi and another
of Livingstone's wood cutters, Amoda. He also brought four
Indian buffalos from Bombay, hoping that they might prove
immune to the tsetse that killed oxen, along with camels, mules
and donkeys from Zanzibar.

"Now that I am on the point of starting on another trip into
Africa," he wrote in his journal, "I feel quite exhilarated." He
looked forward to the "mere animal pleasure of travelling in
a wild unexplored country" – the brisk exercise and sense of
well-being and fitness that it brought, "the stimulus of remote
chances of danger", and the community of "humble hardy
companions". And beyond such bodily pleasures, he said, there
was the idea that ennobled every action on the journey: the
thought that he was an ambassador introducing east Africans to
the British people "by whose agency their land will yet become
enlightened and freed from the slave-trade".

The reality of the expedition quickly fell below his expectation.
Following the heavily wooded north bank of the Rovuma,

they were slowed by constant woodcutting to make way for the animals. Livingstone was appalled by the way the sepoys and Nasik students overburdened and abused them, but when he rebuked their cruelty, they simply rebuked his cruelty in bringing them to this wild place. He could not control what they did when he was not looking, and gave up trying. The David Livingstone who led this expedition seems a milder and weaker man than the one who had led the Makololo for 3,500 miles and fired his way through his Zambezi crew, a man without the energy for command. For the first time in his life, Livingstone found himself falling behind and slowing progress. By the time they reached the savannah uplands in the second week of May, they had lost two camels to disease and/or mistreatment, and four other animals were badly hurt.

Livingstone left the sepoys and Nasik students with the luggage and went with the others to find food, but the region had been devastated by slave raids after a bad harvest. They stayed with Matumora, a chief of the Matambwe, who fed them generously from his meagre remains, and told them stories of attacks. Livingstone was still concerned enough about evangelism to talk to those he met about God, compiling their responses into a religious survey. Matumora told him that the Matambwe prayed to God but did not know or talk much about him. Livingstone said that the British love to talk about him, but concluded that the Matambwe were too reverent to overuse his name. Other chiefs he met in the region had similarly minimalistic religion, one telling him that they knew God existed and was not good because he killed so many people.

Livingstone summoned the sepoys to join him in June, but they refused, until he threatened to send them back. Perhaps having been recruited as soldiers they resented being treated as porters, but he could no longer even make them carry their own things. They crossed a desolate plain where they saw a dead body and heard about a Muslim slaving party, and the next day the twenty-four porters from the coast quit, for fear of slavers. Livingstone had to recruit local porters from town to town to fill their place. By mid-June, he had few animals capable of carrying anything. Eventually six of the sepoys became so disruptive that he tried to punish them by sentencing them to carry some of the loads that as far as he was concerned they were supposed to be carrying anyway. One had twenty pounds of tea and threw away three-quarters of it to lighten his burden.

Livingstone noted the many ruined villages they passed, littered with skulls. Elsewhere they saw large numbers of "slave-taming sticks" dropped in the road, because – so locals told him – the captors were convinced slaves had given up trying to escape; Livingstone thought it more likely they had been liberated by locals so they could resell them. There were also the bodies of those who had failed to keep up and been shot, stabbed or tied to trees and left to die by the Arabs, so that other traders should not profit. Others they found still alive, still wearing the sticks to their necks, dumped because traders could not feed them. Livingstone rescued one highborn woman who was captured while walking between villages and bound by a local man who had not yet had chance to sell her. Traders came while Livingstone was there, but he bought her freedom.

He protested with the chiefs he met who were selling their people. They were delighted that he wanted to stop the slave trade, but astonished when he said they shared responsibility for it in the eyes of God. He suggested they make their money by farming more extensively, but was told that if they did so their crops would merely be taken by nearby tribes. Food was so scarce it was all Livingstone could do to get enough food day by day to keep his men moving, and he paid ruinous amounts of calico for it, not least because they already had as much of the cloth as they could want from slave traders.

Livingstone had planned to go round the north end of Lake Nyasa, but hearing horror stories of the devastation and famine caused by slave wars, he decided to go to the east shore and hitch a ride across the lake on an Arab dhow. It was a desperately slow, ill-disciplined and hungry march. On 14 July, he met a caravan of sixty Muslim slave traders led by one Sef Rupia, and showed him his letter of recommendation from the Sultan. In contrast to the chiefs Livingstone had come to protect, Sef was able to provide him and all his men with an abundance of meat and flour. He also escorted Livingstone to the town of the powerful Chief Mataka near the east coast of Nyasa, then went back to feed and help his straggling sepoys. Livingstone was aware of the paradox involved in receiving such invaluable kindness from the enemy, but he was even more struck by their enviable discipline, writing wistfully about the contrast between his "wretched escort" and the complex divisions of the slaver caravan, "all bound to obey their leader".

They stayed two weeks with Mataka, feeding up, and Livingstone wrote up the geology of the area they had been through. When the sepoys eventually arrived he found they had killed the buffalo calf for food and the donkey because they got it stuck in mud, and had threatened to kill the Nasik students too. He finally sent them back, paying a Muslim slaver to escort them, but allowed their havildar to stay, thinking that though he was a drag on the expedition he would be useful in an emergency.

Leaving Mataka's for the lake, Livingstone was gratified to find smaller slave parties fleeing before them once again, but discovered the disadvantage of his reputation when he reached Nyasa: "All flee from me as if I had the plague, and I cannot in consequence transmit letters to the coast, or get across the Lake." This, he later told Frere, was "lest I should burn them as slavers!" So they walked round the south of the lake instead.

He took a detour to visit Chief Mukate and try to dissuade him from selling slaves, describing the horrific scenes they had witnessed along the way. Mukate said that Arab traders had told him that Livingstone was capturing slavers and their slaves simply to take possession of them himself. After a long talk Livingstone felt his arguments had hit home, and the guide Mukate gave him spread the same message to the villages they passed through.

In Chief Mponda's town, they found a party of six mixed-race slavers from Zanzibar. Promising not to make a scene, Livingstone took the chance to inspect their cargo: eighty-five slaves, mostly boys, locked in a pen and secured by the neck. The traders told him they made little money from the work – the profits were all in Zanzibar. Other Muslim slave parties fled at their coming, and Livingstone reflected bitterly that on the waters the *Lady Nyassa* was meant to patrol, slave dhows ruled the waves. Around the Shire, the familiar landscape was now scattered with skulls and bones. "One would fain not notice them, but they are so striking as one trudges along the sultry path, that it cannot be avoided."

In September, Livingstone resorted to caning one of the Nasik students, Andrew Powell, for "skulking" – weakness did not make him always milder – and he left the expedition. The Yao crewman Wakatiki met his brother and left the expedition to be reunited with the family that had sold him into slavery. The havildar quit the following day. Days later they met an Arab slaver coming the opposite way who said that forty-four of his party had been killed by Mazitu (or Ngoni) raiders, at which news the ten Johanna men quit. Six months and 500 miles into the journey, and Livingstone's crew of sixty was reduced to ten: the remaining Nasik students plus Chuma, Susi and Amoda.

At the south-western tip of the lake, Livingstone met Chief Kimsusa of the Manganja, an old friend from the Zambezi expedition. He fed them well, loaded them with gifts and provisions, and better still from Livingstone's point of view, said the reason his town was three times as big as when Livingstone last saw it was that he had followed his advice not to sell slaves.

Livingstone revived his old vocation of preaching to some of the tribes, but now the main thrust of his sermons was urging them to believe that all people are children of God and so should not be sold.

In October they met a large village running in terror from the approaching Mazitu army. Livingstone and his company prepared to fight the Mazitu in defence of their own possessions and the villagers, but the army turned away to the south shortly before reaching them.

In December they met two escaped Yao slaves who said – though Livingstone doubted them – that their master had been killed by Mazitu, and they wanted to join the expedition. Livingstone was in two minds, but agreed: "In general, runaway slaves are bad characters, but these two seem good men, and we want them to fill up our complement." Heading north-west into what is now Zambia, he crossed the Loangwa, the major river which flows from Lake Malawi into the Zambezi. To the north, he found the people hostile, unwilling to provide guides, food or shelter.

Along with the thought that 1866 had "not been so fruitful or useful as I intended", New Year 1867 brought heavy rain, and more hunger, the wildlife having migrated as well as the people:

> *I feel always hungry, and am constantly dreaming of*
> *better food when I should be sleeping…*
> *   It is not the unpleasantness of eating unpalatable*
> *food that teases one, but we are never satisfied…*
> *   I took my belt up three holes to relieve hunger…* [24]

He met people living on mushrooms and leaves, and bought rancid elephant meat to eat with indigestible millet, finding each took the edge off the other's deficiencies.

But the worst was most decidedly yet to be.

Chapter 22

MISERY

On 20 January 1867, in what is today Zambia, Livingstone and his crew walked from the village of Lisunga on the River Lobo into forest, and there the two Yao ex-slaves ran off with the loads they were carrying. Livingstone gave chase but the forest was thick and a heavy shower covered the thieves' tracks. They had taken their flour, dishes, tools, two guns, a lot of gunpowder and, what alarmed Livingstone more than all the rest put together, his entire supply of medicine. He tried to console himself with the conviction that anything God allows to happen is for the best, but it was not easy. He also pleaded the thieves' cause in his journal with a liberality that contrasts starkly with his judgments on British men who had crossed him in earlier times: their life of slavery had given them small chance to learn honour or honesty, yet they behaved impeccably for seven weeks before hunger, fatigue and rain wore them down. "True," he concluded; "yet this loss of the medicine-box gnaws at the heart terribly."

Livingstone continued on his way without the medicines. His reasons for this decision have been lengthily discussed, but his biographer George Seaver hits the nail on the head: "It was no decision, for it is quite certain that no other idea entered his mind." A porter dropped and damaged his chronometer, which made his longitude readings and mapping incorrect from this point, and later that year an earthquake damaged it even more. Hunger still preoccupied him. "We all feel weak and easily tired," he wrote, "and an incessant hunger teases us… real biting hunger and faintness." "In changing my dress this morning I was frightened at my own emaciation." He dreamed of roast beef and woke to find his pillow wet with drool.

Eighty miles south of Lake Tanganyika, though, they came
to Chief Chitapangwa's, and he gave them an ox, hippo meat,
and plenty of cereal. Almost as welcome, a Muslim slave party
stopped en route to Zanzibar, and agreed, for a consideration,
to take letters there, and wait for a day while he wrote them.
He sent a report describing the slave trade to Lord Clarendon,
the Foreign Secretary, and to Bartle Frere. He wrote to Agnes,
"My Darling Nannie", to Murchison, and to George Seward,
the acting Consul in Zanzibar. He told Seward, "I am a mere
ruckle of bones," and asked him to send supplies to Ujiji, an
Arab town 360 miles north on the east shore of Tanganyika,
listing medicine, food, coffee, port, candles and sealing wax.

He also wrote to Reverend Norman McLeod, the journalist,
founder of the Evangelical Alliance and mission organizer
for the Church of Scotland, renewing his plans for founding
mission stations. They had talked on Livingstone's last furlough
of McLeod sending German missionaries, as the CMS had done
to Sierra Leone, and Livingstone now recommended Mataka's
town to the east of Lake Nyasa, as temperate, high, well-
watered, and good for growing peas.

Chitapangwa did not allow Livingstone to leave for three
weeks, demanding one of his blankets in payment for his
hospitality. Livingstone tried to explain, with his usual mix of
common sense and bravado, that they all belonged to the Nasik
students, so he had no right to give them nor Chitapangwa
to ask for them; but they had to use the students themselves
as interpreters, and Livingstone eventually discovered they had
been toning down the argument both ways. "In their cringing
souls they believe they know what should be said better than
I do. It does not strike them in the least that I have grown
grey amongst these people." Once he managed to talk in his
own words he and Chitapangwa became friends. Livingstone
shared his faith with him and, having no magic lantern, showed
him pictures from Smith's *Bible Dictionary*. He left on friendly
enough terms for Chitapangwa to give him a knife.

Livingstone suffered from malaria throughout March 1867 but his only remedy was to press on, crossing the Losauswa Mountains and making the steep descent to Lake Tanganyika, arriving on 1 April. He was enraptured by its beauty, but within days fever seized him so violently he could not even get into his hut. His men carried him in and hung a rug over the doorway to hide him.

It took a month for Livingstone to recover. Then he wanted to go north around the lake to explore its west coast, and to "discover" Lake Mweru (or Moero), which lay 160 miles west of Tanganyika and sounded like part of the watershed on which Murchison wanted him to report. However, Livingstone and his men were turned back by warnings of a war between the Tabwa chief Nsama and Zanzibari slave traders. Taking cover, he met Hamis Wodim Tagh, a slaver sent by one of the largest trading companies in Zanzibar; Livingstone showed him the Sultan's letter and asked him for information. Hamis complied, gave Livingstone food, cloth and beads, and cared for them all while they were stuck there for months. When Hamis visited Nsama and successfully negotiated peace, Livingstone was impressed, saying, "These Zanzibar men are very different from the slavers of the Waiyau [Yao] country."

Still, Hamis brought fresh slaves back from the journey. He told Livingstone they were taken from villages that fought to stop him reaching Nsama, and would be returned when Nsama paid a debt of ivory. Nevertheless Livingstone watched a woman and her three-year-old son being sold separately, for two yards and four yards of calico respectively. "He understood it all," noted Livingstone, "and cried bitterly, clinging to his mother. She had, of course, no power to help him... Slavery is a great evil wherever I have seen it."

The peace being formalized by each party drinking the other's blood (diluted in a lot of water), Hamis took Livingstone's party to Lake Mweru. Thus, and not for the last time, Livingstone found himself in the incongruous position of being escorted and provisioned on his abolitionist trek by the very dealers in human beings whose trade he was attempting to destroy. This awkward fact might be glossed, as George Seaver argued quite reasonably, as Livingstone's taking what he wanted from the slavers and using it against them, in the same way that slave traders had taken advantage of his earlier expeditions to promote the slave trade. He also gained invaluable information about the trade. The problem is that he also became surprisingly friendly with several of them, and at least once gave them vital help. Ultimately though, the only alternative to coming to friendly terms with the enemy would have been to abandon the expedition altogether, and if Livingstone believed that its achievements would be more important than the taint of compromise, he was right.

They arrived at Lake Mweru on 8 November. It was the first recorded European sighting of the lake which today lies on the border of Zambia and the Democratic Republic of the Congo, and Livingstone was thrilled to hear that the River Lualaba flowed into its south end and out of its north, connecting it both ways with other lakes. This chain of lakes was the watershed he was looking for, and it also seemed to be the head waters of a major river – it was in fact the Congo. Wanting to trace the river southwards to the higher Lake Bangweulu (or Bemba), Livingstone set off with his crew.

He stopped at Kazembe for information, and took an instant dislike to the chief Mwata Kazembe VII. His gate was decorated with sixty human skulls, and many of his people were missing hands or part of their ears, cut off as punishment. He had an executioner who wore ear-scissors round his neck, and a dwarf jester. Livingstone tried as usual to dissuade the chief from selling slaves, but he cut him off with a speech about how great his town was. Livingstone believed the population had been decimated by his cruelty and unpopularity.

Livingstone and his men were given all the fish and flour they could manage. They were also fed by two Arab–African traders who were there, Mohammad bin Saleh and Mohammad Bogharib. The latter, a notoriously ruthless slave-turned-slaver, had a huge consignment of captives and gave Livingstone food containing the first honey or sugar he had tasted in over a year. "It nauseated from its horrible sweetness," he said. He also gave Livingstone some paper, on which he wrote a despatch to the Foreign Secretary, saying, "If one wished to depict the slave-trade in its most attractive, or rather least objectionable, form, he would accompany these gentlemen subjects of the Sultan of Zanzibar."

They left in December 1867, and only afterwards did Livingstone realize that bin Saleh had been a prisoner in Kazembe for ten years, and was freed to resume his trading career thanks to the letter Livingstone bore from the Sultan. Livingstone explored Mweru again and saw the Lualaba exit it to the north, naming it Webb's River after the family who put him up in Newstead Abbey. But the way to Lake Bangweulu was such an ordeal of rain and malarial swamps that six of his ten men left him to accompany bin Saleh to Ujiji, and it was all Livingstone could do to keep four: Chuma, Susi, Amoda and the Nasik student, Gardner. Susi and Chuma had relationships with women attached to bin Saleh's caravan. "Susi stood like a mule," he writes in an understandably unpublished section of his journal. "I put my hand on his arm... he seized my hand, and refused to let it go. When he did I fired a pistol at him, but missed. There being no law or magistrate higher than myself, I would not be thwarted." This treatment of one of his "faithfuls" is the low point in Livingstone's dealings with African people, and understandably did not make it into the published version of his last journals. His comment on the others, two days later, did: "I did not blame them very severely in my own mind for absconding: they were tired of tramping, and so verily am I."

Livingstone, Chuma, Susi, Amoda, and Gardner trudged through long grass, foul-smelling waterlogged plains and thick black mud. On the Luongo on 24 June 1868, they saw traders

with six slaves who seemed to be singing happily. Livingstone
translated the verse with some help:

> *"Oh, you sent me off to Manga (sea-coast), but the
> yoke is off when I die, and back I shall come to haunt
> and to kill you." Then all joined in the chorus, which
> was the name of each vendor. It told not of fun, but of
> the bitterness and tears of such as were oppressed, and
> on the side of the oppressors there was a power: there
> be higher than they!* [25]

They reached Lake Bangweulu on 18 July. Livingstone visited
the islands, wrote a detailed report on the region and talked
to the people about the fatherhood of God and the evil of the
slave trade. Not having heard a word from friends or family in
more than two years, he wrote wistfully to Oswell: "In looking
back to Kolobeng I have one regret, and that is that I did not
feel it my duty to play with my children as much as to teach the
Bakwains. I worked very hard at that, and was tired out at night.
Now I have none to play with. So, my good friend, play while
you may." He also wrote to Agnes: "I broke my teeth tearing
maize and other hard food, and they are coming out. One front
tooth is out, and I have such an awful mouth! If you expect a
kiss from me, you must take it through a speaking-trumpet."
He soon had to pull out all his front teeth.

Desperate for news from home, Livingstone headed north
towards Ujiji, and met up again with bin Saleh and Bogharib.
But now a new and greater war had broken out, involving
Kazembe and Mazitu raiders, as well as Nsama and the Arabs.
On 22 November their own caravan and that of their local
allies, the Banyamwezi, came under attack for three days by
the Babemba tribe. Livingstone was much more impressed with
the courage of the Babemba attackers than the Arab gunmen,
reckoning that only the Banyamwezi saved them. He told

Bogharib the whole thing was his fault, for seizing Babemba women to replace four runaway slaves, and persuaded him to return them.

When they continued, Livingstone marched separately from the Muslims, but kept in contact. He was constantly soaked by rain and rivers, and ate poorly. In the first week of 1869 he brought up blood from his lungs, "my strongest part", and found he had pneumonia. Bogharib arranged for him to be carried the rest of the way, and gave him medicine, but had little food to share. His feet swelled, he slept badly, got seriously sunburnt, grew alarmingly thin again and found maggots in his arms and legs. It seemed unlikely that he would survive another 300 miles like this around the north shore of Tanganyika, so it was arranged for canoeists belonging to one of the greatest slave traders of all, Said bin Habib, to carry him across, via the islands.

It took a week to cross the lake, into what is today Tanzania, and in another day Livingstone finally reached Ujiji to collect his long-awaited supplies from the Consul at Zanzibar, to revive his body and his expedition. All that was waiting for him there was a shock.

Chapter 23

UJIJI TO THE LUALABA

When he arrived at Ujiji on 14 March 1869, Livingstone was expecting cheese and preserved meats, wine, coffee and quinine, live buffalos, and cloth and beads to buy more, and letters and newspapers. Instead he found that his food, medicine and any papers had been delivered to Unyanyembe (called Tabora today), 250 miles east on the other side of a Mazitu war. Only 2,000 yards of cloth had got through, three-quarters of which was then stolen along with most of the beads. The buffalos all died en route. His coffee was there, and a P&O inspector gave him tea, but there was no milk in town. Livingstone greeted the calamity with an upper lip of steel: "I found great benefit from the tea and coffee, and still more from flannel to the skin."

Livingstone recuperated, cared for by Chuma, Susi, Amoda and Gardner. He wrote forty-two letters in six weeks, but found it hard to persuade anyone going to Zanzibar to deliver them, and when someone did take them, they were almost all destroyed. This was because the Sultan, while allowing the buying and selling of slaves, forbade his people to capture them, and the Ujijians feared Livingstone was reporting their extensive slave taking. Which, of course, is exactly what Livingstone was doing. In his journal, he described Ujiji as "a den of the worst kind of slave-traders... the vilest of the vile. It is not a trade, but a system of consecutive murders; they go to plunder and kidnap, and every trading trip is nothing but a foray."

In May, Mohammad bin Saleh arrived in Ujiji and secured an empty house for Livingstone. Within a fortnight, he was feeling well enough for his next geographical expedition. Some said that a river flowed out of the north end of Lake Tanganyika, which sounded to Livingstone like a source of the Nile, and he hoped that the string of lakes to the west along the Lualaba, including the Mweru, would prove to be another one, though he feared it might only be the Congo. In truth, the Lualaba is a source of the Congo, and the river that drains Tanganyika flows out not to the north but the west; it is called the Lukuga and it joins the Lualaba, making another source of the Congo. It leaves the lake at the point where Livingstone was paddled across en route to Ujiji just weeks previously, but unluckily he had been too ill to notice this crucial fact. There was no source of the Nile to be found here, but finding it was becoming Livingstone's most fervent hope, so he planned a trip to investigate the Lualaba by canoe.

Ujiji was too hostile to provide any porters for Livingstone, but Mohammad Bogharib turned up and agreed to take him to the Lualaba. They crossed Tanganyika in July 1869, landing fifteen miles from the unnoticed Lukuga outlet. Bogharib fed Livingstone well, but he found himself out of breath on the gentlest slopes and suffered from dysentery and bleeding piles. He persuaded Bogharib to let some of his slaves walk without their taming sticks, and one being near home ran away. Livingstone was disgusted to hear their local guide planning to catch him for the reward.

Halfway to the Lualaba, they came to the village of Bambarre in the Manyema region, which the Arabs used as a trading base, and Bogharib left Livingstone and his little band there. Again he could get no guides or porters at Bambarre to take him further into Manyema, so he waited and rested and wrote letters. He reported on his geographical work with an irresistibly growing confidence that after groping around in the dark for lack of help he had discovered the source of the Nile.

Writing to his son Tom, David celebrated the victory of the anti-slavery army in the USA: "War has elevated and purified the Yankees, and now they have the gigantic task laid at their doors to elevate and purify 4,000,000 of slaves. I earnestly hope that the Northerners may not be found wanting in their portion of the superhuman work. The day for Africa is yet to come." Recalling the mood of paternal repentance in which he had talked to Oswell, David told Tom, "I sometimes feel greatly distressed about you, and if I could be of any use I would leave my work unfinished to aid you." He told him that he would not live long and had little to bequeath him but his honour. In fact he had less than he thought: unknown to Livingstone the Indian bank where he had deposited the £2,300 he made from selling the *Ma-Robert* had collapsed and he had lost it all.

Feeling better, and tired of waiting, Livingstone left Bambarre with his crew on 1 November. He was going further from the east coast into central Africa than any European had yet been. In fact, even the Arabs had only just entered the region, on a trading expedition led by the most powerful slave trader of all, Dugumbe of Ujiji. Livingstone had met Dugumbe on his way back to Ujiji in September, carrying eight tons of ivory. After Dugumbe's foray of robbery and murder, Livingstone faced deep suspicion at Manyema villages. The few whom Dugumbe had not reached were friendly, but most refused even to take Livingstone's band to the next village. They reached the Lualaba, but no one would sell them a canoe, so they were forced to return to Bambarre.

There Mohammad Bogharib was waiting for him. He told Livingstone that a horde of 500 Ujijian gunmen had just passed into Manyema, inspired by Dugumbe's fantastic spoils and the fact that a cholera epidemic then decimating the slave population of Zanzibar had raised prices irresistibly. Bogharib gave Livingstone a goat to cook for Christmas dinner, and they headed back towards the Lualaba together on Boxing Day.

Taking a more northerly route this time, they found the locals had never met traders and were perfectly welcoming. Their curiosity could be rather overwhelming though, and frightened Bogharib's men, who had heard the Manyema people were cannibals. Livingstone scorned this rumour at first, offering a reward to anyone who found evidence, but he later came to believe it, meeting a man who said he ate those he killed in battle: "Human flesh," said he, "is better than goat's – saltish and even peppery."

Livingstone's bleeding, dysentery and malaria were joined by cholera. He was slowed down by weakness, tiredness and fear of the consequences of getting too wet. Nevertheless, he forded rivers and swamps waist deep and endured numerous downpours, but when they reached yet another mud channel on 7 February 1870 Livingstone felt too ill to face it, and took shelter at the Arab station at Mamohela with his helpers while Bogharib went on.

Livingstone stayed there for four months, in which time Amoda finally quit. Livingstone, Susi, Chuma and Gardner set off towards the Lualaba again in June, in conditions that make it astonishing that anyone at all should have stayed with him. They forded up to fourteen streams a day, thigh deep, each with forty yards of mud on either side. "Trees fallen across the path formed a breast-high wall which had to be climbed over: flooded rivers, breast and neck deep, had to be crossed, the mud was awful, and nothing but villages eight or ten miles apart." On top of all this, having no decent shoes, "irritable-eating ulcers fastened on both feet; and I limped back to Bambarré on 22nd".

Laid up back in Mamohela, the agony of his feet was a source of abolitionist reflections: "The wailing", he noted in his journal, "of the slaves tortured with these sores is one of the night sounds of a slave-camp: they eat through everything – muscle, tendon, and bone, and often lame permanently if they do not kill the poor things." Only after thirty slaves there died of the disease did someone tell him a cure – powdered malachite applied with a feather – which gradually restored his feet. He spent the rest of the year in Bambarre waiting for one of his friends with their slave-taking platoons to bring supplies and letters and to help him get to the Lualaba. His writings while he waited contained romantic visions of finding the legendary city of Moses as well as the source of the Nile, and a longing to be spared long enough to complete his geographical work. He was angrily disappointed when Chuma and Gardner joined an Arab raid, the latter returning with a woman.

Finally, on 4 February 1871, a crew of seven men came for Livingstone with supplies. They had been sent by Kirk, who was now Acting Consul at Zanzibar, and once again Livingstone was painfully disappointed. He was happy to hear that Kirk was alive, having been told he had died in the cholera epidemic. Likewise, Kirk was happy to hear that Livingstone was alive: the ten Johanna men who had quit the expedition in 1866 avoided getting into trouble for deserting him by reporting that Livingstone had been murdered at Lake Nyasa. Kirk had flown the flag at half-mast, and the Foreign Secretary had sent a naval expedition up the Shire to investigate – which not only heard news that he was still alive, but in the process got a steamer past the Murchison Cataracts onto Lake Nyasa, as Livingstone had never quite managed, in one attempt. But of all the supplies that Kirk had sent now, only tea, coffee and quinine arrived. The rest were in Ujiji, being enjoyed by the two men who were supposed to be leading the crew, Sherif and Awathe. In return Livingstone sent Kirk a cheque from his non-existent bank account. The men had brought letters from Waller and Kirk. Waller sent an 1869 copy of *The Standard*, telling Livingstone he would leave the writing of other news to Kirk, as he soon expected Livingstone to emerge at the mouth of the Nile, which brought a long bitter retort from Livingstone. From Kirk's letter, Livingstone was dismayed to learn that just one of the forty-two letters he had written in Ujiji had reached Zanzibar, but that one counted: it gave Kirk an account of the slave trade, which he forwarded to Frere, and they both used it to put pressure on the British government and the Sultan to do something about Zanzibar slaving.

The men Kirk sent worked for the largest Banian trading house, Banians being Zanzibaris of Indian descent. It was the organization the English Consulate generally used, having no workforce of its own, but Zanzibar being a society built on slavery, the majority of Livingstone's team now consisted of slaves. They were paid for the expedition, but were unenthusiastic. They told Livingstone they were under orders not to accompany him to the Lualaba but to bring him back to Zanzibar. This was not true, and the letter disproved it, but it still took Bogharib's threatening to shoot them for the Lualaba trip to start.

Chapter 24

MASSACRE

Livingstone found both the people and the scenery of the Manyema region in southern Congo very attractive. He wrote lyrically of the delightful scenes of women baking and kids gambolling in the delicious air, suggesting sardonically that such memories might explain the mystery of why slaves run away home. But the depredations of the Muslim slave traders were starting to destroy the region. "The way in which they murder the men and seize the women and children makes me sick at heart," he wrote to Agnes. "It is not slave-trade. It is murdering free people to make slaves. It is perfectly indescribable." He had made an important discovery, that though the east African slave trade was smaller than the west, the human cost was immeasurable because of the policy of murdering whole villages to take some of the women and children. Yet his sole journal entry for 20 March 1871 was: "I am heartsore, and sick of human blood."

Livingstone ran out of notepaper for his journal, and on 23 March he cut up the eight pages of *The Standard* Waller had sent to make two little thirty-two-page notebooks, writing at right angles to the newsprint to make it more legible. In April he ran out of ink too, but made his own from seeds used in Manyema for cloth dye. The following year, in Ujiji, he wrote them up, extensively editing them, and after his death, Waller used the later version as the basis for *The Last Journals of David Livingstone*, covering the whole expedition. The originals survived, becoming illegible as the ink faded, but the text was recovered in 2011 by spectral imaging thanks to the David Livingstone Spectral Imaging Project. The account of the next six months, perhaps the most significant months in Livingstone's life, is taken mostly from there.

On 28 March, Livingstone wrote, "So many difficulties have been put in my way I doubt whether the Divine favour and will is on my side." But two days later he reached the Lualaba, at Nyangwe, a large market town of the Bagenya tribe and the westernmost Muslim trading station. The Arabs had been there ten years and forced many of the Bagenya into settlements across the river. Livingstone heard that the Lualaba tended westwards from there, which would mean it was probably not the Nile after all, so he wanted to buy a canoe to see whether this was true, but once again found that fear of the Arabs made it impossible. "The Manyema have learned to distrust all strangers, and think to buy means plunder and murder." Livingstone considered this a reasonable conclusion from their experience but was annoyed to find the Banian slaves telling local people that he did indeed plan to kill them. The "Banians" (as Livingstone called them, though they were African slaves of the Banians) turned out to be thugs. They beat and robbed people going to market, and Livingstone paid compensation, saying, "I am sick at heart in knowing of these outrages." When the Arabs asked for help in a confrontation with local people, he refused to send them, saying, "If they go anywhere I must go with them or murder is certain."

Livingstone loved the market, which was held every fourth day and brought more than a thousand people, buying and selling pots, cassava, grass, cloth, oil, ironware, fish and fowls. He took a house on the square and counted the people passing his door. "It seems a pleasure of life to haggle and joke and laugh and cheat..." he wrote. "Bought two fishes with long snouts – very good eating."

Livingstone became friends with an Arab slave trader in Nyangwe called Abed, who won his heart by saying he had been persuaded by his preaching against bloodshed and ordered his men "to give presents to the chiefs and not kill unless attacked". Like Livingstone, Abed wanted to go down the Lualaba, in search of ivory, so he negotiated with a nearby chief, Kalenga, for a pair of canoes. Livingstone was delighted to be setting an example of fair trade, but the process took three months and cost him a thousand shells, three goats and some beads, and in the end there were no canoes. The supposed seller refused to return Livingstone's payment to him, having received it from Abed – who meanwhile had repaired another canoe and left in it.

At first Livingstone was content to leave the matter with Abed, but his resentment grew. Five days later, on 9 June, he reflected on his cheating in his journal, but added, "I must not be the first to do what may be called injustice. The Arabs would like to see me using force." However, on 13 June, he sent his incorrigible Banians "to force Kalenga to reason – if he refuses to refund, to bind and give him a flogging". Kalenga and his people fled from them, Livingstone got nothing, and had to stay. This account is taken from Livingstone's *Standard* journal; the brief version of the incident which appeared in Livingstone's fair copy of the journal later was less explicit: "when I sent to force him to give up the goods, all his village fled into the forest."

He heard two weeks later that the Arab expedition that had gone up the river without him had hit a whirlpool; the leading canoe and its crew were lost and the expedition turned back. "It is in answer to my prayers that I have been mercifully prevented from going down river," concluded Livingstone, "for I would have been the leading canoe."

Nevertheless, he still wanted a canoe, even if it was just to cross the river, and now a new source of help was at hand. Two of the greatest slave traders in east Africa, fervently awaited by Livingstone in case they brought letters for him, arrived in Nyangwe. One was Said bin Habib, whose canoes had saved his life by carrying him across Tanganyika to Ujiji; the other was Dugumbe, who had opened the western region to traders. Dugumbe settled outside Nyangwe with 500 gunmen, and presented Livingstone with eighty large strings of beads. Livingstone asked him to send for what was left of his looted goods at Ujiji.

Dugumbe confirmed Livingstone's suspicions that the Banian slaves were spreading rumours about him to stop him travelling further, and agreed to help him get a canoe. But then the Banian slaves informed him they would only go with him for the first leg of the journey, and when Livingstone said they would get no more pay if they refused to work, they replied that they would never work for someone who was too scared to beat them. So Livingstone implored Dugumbe for ten men to replace them. Livingstone offered him a cheque for £400 plus every scrap of his possessions that were still at Ujiji or might be reclaimed there from the thieves (one of whom, he heard, had taken to wearing his chronometer), "only don't let me be forced to return to Ujiji so near the end of my work". Dugumbe said he would have to consult.

Meanwhile, Livingstone was distressed to see Arab warfare coming closer than ever. Manilla, a leading gunman slave of Said bin Habib, had made an alliance with the Bagenya people across the river to attack and enslave their neighbours, and on 29 June Livingstone counted ten villages of "our market people" burning. Apart from anything, Livingstone deplored the Bagenya's shortsightedness: if the villages banded together they could mount a formidable defence against the invaders, but instead they betrayed their neighbours, leaving themselves without help when the invaders turned on them.

A week later, the Bagenya chief, Kimburu, visited Dugumbe and made a new alliance with him. It did not help. Throughout the morning of 15 July 1871, Livingstone heard Dugumbe's gunmen across the river, killing Kimburu and others, taking Bagenya slaves, and burning another twelve villages. "And so it goes on," he wrote in his newsprint journal, "making me fear to go with Dugumbe's people to be partakers in their blood guiltiness."

This time, however, it went on a lot further. It was market day, and despite the war 1,500 people came. Late in the morning,

Livingstone saw three of Dugumbe's men carrying guns and considered telling them off as guns were not allowed in the market, but it was a hot sultry day and he decided to go back indoors instead. One of the three started arguing over a chicken, and then the gunfire started.

It quickly became a massacre. Villagers dropped everything and ran for the river, but the three men kept firing on them, and more gunmen joined them. Many villagers could not get their jumble of boats out of the creek in time to escape; many jumped into the water and drowned. Even some of those who reached the other bank were shot by gunmen there. In his room, Livingstone wrote, "It is awful – terrible – a dreadful world this – As I write shot after shot falls on the fugitives on the other side who are wailing loudly over those they know are already slain. Oh let thy kingdom come." He wrote, for the first time in three months, in real ink, as if he had kept a last drop in reserve for a story that could not be allowed to fade.

For hours the women of Nyangwe collected the goods dropped by refugees. Livingstone found nineteen people who had escaped downstream in the water and got them to friends. He found Dugumbe himself "and proposed to catch the bloodhounds who fired in the chitoka [market] and on the canoes, and put their heads on poles". But Dugumbe was not interested and just blamed Manilla.

The following morning, Livingstone briskly noted, he spent "liberating [the] captured", reuniting more than thirty with husbands and friends before they could be enslaved. At midday there was more shooting and the burning of yet more villages from Dugumbe's men across the river. An hour later they were sailing back, beating drums in triumph, while women cheered them home and comrades fired in salute.

Hundreds had been killed. The Arabs reckoned 350 to 400 people. Dugumbe denied instigating the atrocity and Livingstone seemed to believe him, noting that he had taken in some refugees and then released them, without being asked, rather than keeping them as slaves. The attack was led by his Muslim follower Tagamoio, who took twenty-seven slaves, and did not get his head on a spike or face any other repercussions either. He explained the motivation of the attack to Livingstone, saying that "he went to punish the friends of Manilla who being a slave had no right to make war and burn villages".

There was no question now of heading west with Dugumbe's militia. Livingstone wanted to leave them at the first opportunity. "This open murder fills me with unspeakable horror – and I wish to get away from it." The day after the massacre, Dugumbe met with the attacked chiefs, professed friendship, realizing, Livingstone says, that the attack had been a bad idea. The chiefs appealed to Livingstone to stay, but even if it could have done any good, he could not bear it.

He could not continue north down the river, as his Banian slaves had already refused, so on 17 July he told them he wanted to go south towards the river source, but they refused that too, so the only choice left was to accept defeat and walk 300 miles back to Ujiji.

He spent the next day in his room, tormented by the "unspeakable horror" he had seen. He had a headache and copious bleeding. The following day was market day, and a fraction of the usual numbers came, including Bagenya merchants bringing salt to try to buy back the baskets they had dropped last time.

Dugumbe gave Livingstone leaving presents of a good goat, gunpowder and a profusion of beads and shells. Livingstone asked him to sell him a sample of Bagenya workmanship, and Dugumbe sent two swords and two spears, telling Livingstone there was no charge, but Livingstone sent two fine cloths, "as he had no cloth and is very friendly". The next day, with Susi, Chuma, Gardner and the slaves, he started the seven-week walk back to Ujiji.

When Livingstone's account of the Nyangwe massacre reached Britain – first by letter, then through Stanley's *How I Found Livingstone*, then in Waller's edition of his *Last Journals* – the shockwaves were tremendous and it became perhaps the most notorious and influential event of his life. The immediate unconsidered notes of his *Standard* journal take us much closer to Livingstone's actual experience than any of those accounts, making its recovery by the Spectral Imaging Project invaluable.

It was published, however, by the project director Adrian S. Wisnicki as *Livingstone's 1871 Field Diary: A multispectral critical edition*, which went beyond textual recovery to offer a radical reinterpretation of the event that was widely reported, for example, as "Dr Livingstone 'lied in famous account of slave market massacre'" in *The Daily Telegraph*.

Wisnicki's contention is that the original *Standard* journal reveals "Livingstone's slaves had a part in inciting the Nyangwe massacre"; that because they were his men he was culpable, and so when he wrote up the later version he distanced the slaves from the massacre and generally presented them in a better light, to cover the truth that he himself "helped occasion the horrific event".

There is no question that Livingstone could spin a story to avoid bad publicity for his mission. But whether this famous account is false comes down to two questions. First, did the Banian slaves indeed start the massacre? The only evidence that they did is Livingstone's statement in the *Standard* journal: "A worthless Moslem asserted that all was done by the people of the English." This is a flimsy piece of hearsay to overrule all Livingstone's observations before and after this that it was Dugumbe's men, and the evidence that it was a large, orchestrated campaign by them on both sides of the river – a point Livingstone himself makes in his next sentence: "This will spread though the murderers are on the other side plundering and shooting." The slander of Livingstone's bloodthirstiness was already well established, so it is easy to see why the Muslims would blame him and why the Bagenya would believe them; less easy to see why anyone would believe them today.

The second question is whether the earlier and later versions of the journal disagree about the involvement and character of the slaves. The later so-called "benign" version agrees with the earlier that they were robbers, liars, "riffraff" and potential killers, but Wisnicki cites three amendments altering their portrayal. The first concerns the line "I must go with them or murder is certain", which "becomes more benign" in its portrayal of them thus: "No matter what charges I gave, my Banian slaves would be sure to shed human blood." This is a slightly milder turn of phrase but the meaning is exactly the same.

Secondly, Wisnicki notes Livingstone's sending the slaves to flog Kalenga because of the undelivered canoe, remarking that the later version of his account is less explicit. This is true, as mentioned above; but it makes more sense as a simple case of Livingstone enhancing his own questionable conduct than as a Machiavellian enhancement of the slaves' conduct, in which case it has nothing to do with the massacre.

The last change is to the accusation itself: "A worthless Moslem asserted that all was done by the people of the English", which becomes in the later version, "Two wretched Moslems asserted 'that the firing was done by the people of the English'. I asked one of them why he lied so and he could utter no excuse." This, it is alleged, makes Livingstone's response to the accusation in the original seem "much more ambiguous", but to be more accurate, in the original he makes no response at all. He would have no reason to include in his own notes an explicit denial of charges he knew were false, especially under the conditions he was writing in; the fact that he then included a denial in the journal he expected to publish is not in itself evidence that the denial was untrue. And if the main thrust of this passage in the later version is to clear the name of his Banian slaves, one wonders why he increased the number of witnesses against them from one to two.

In all then, the publication of Livingstone's *Standard* journal offers a valuable view of a crucial moment in his last years that does not undermine the veracity of his later accounts in the slightest.

Chapter 25

STANLEY

If there was a measure of relief for Livingstone leaving Nyangwe for Ujiji on 20 July 1871, it was a small one. He was leaving the company of murderous slavers, but still saw their work wherever he went. He saw vast numbers of villages burnt by Arab traders or their slaves, sometimes because they had been refused lodging by villagers who knew they would be robbed, sometimes for the fun of it.

After a week, they met an Arab caravan whose leaders wanted to send a consignment of ivory to Ujiji, so Livingstone and his men teamed up with their Manyema porters. Whole villages ran away at their approach, and the porters wanted to plunder their huts, but Livingstone rebuked and threatened them. At one such village the people reappeared to throw stones at the travellers, and a man threw a spear at Livingstone from thirty feet which, incredibly, missed. Livingstone explained: "He was too sure of his aim and the good hand of God was upon me." Within twenty-four hours, the same thing happened again, in an attack which killed two Manyema, and Livingstone also narrowly escaped death from a felled tree.

On 9 August, Livingstone reached the end of his notebook, writing, "I be[came] sick & weary & careless of m[y life]." The end of the page is lost. He wrote the next day's entry not only over the text of *The Standard* but over his own earlier writing, then switched to envelopes.

Livingstone completed the journey to Ujiji suffering severe internal bleeding, violent diarrhoea, weakness and depression. Numerous Arab caravans were converging on the town, he noted. "All the traders were returning successful: I alone had

failed and experienced worry, thwarting, baffling, when almost
in sight of the end towards which I strained."

His plan was to rest and recuperate at Ujiji, using whatever
was left of his goods there to buy food, then assemble a better
crew for his next expedition. He arrived in October (23 October
according to his journal, though he later found he was twenty
days ahead), and discovered that not the least scrap of his things
remained. He was reunited with the "absconder" Amoda, and
fed by the Ujijians and given a house, but the thought of having
to live on their charity made him more miserable than ever. As a
final twist, the thief, Sherif, was still in town, unpunished though
everyone knew what he had done, and shamelessly wished him
good luck, "offered me his hand!!!" and told him he was off to
prayers. (The Arabs Livingstone had travelled with combined
slavery and murder with regular devotions, giving him a bad
impression of Islam.) Livingstone tried to get recompense from
Sherif, but failed.

He was destitute, stranded, 800 miles from the nearest known
British person, with no way to get word out. "My spirits were
at their lowest ebb," he says.

So it was that, on the sixth day of his miserable stay, he was
sitting under his veranda, when a smartly dressed white man in
a pith helmet and riding boots walked up to the house, took
off his hat, and said in an American accent, "Dr Livingstone, I
presume?"

Henry Morton Stanley, a thirty-year-old journalist with *The New
York Herald*, was born John Rowlands in Denbigh in Wales.
He was the illegitimate son of a butcher's daughter and spent
nine of his early years in St Asaph's workhouse. At seventeen he
worked his passage to New Orleans, where he was befriended
and virtually adopted by a plantation owner called Henry Hope
Stanley. Though they fell out a year later, Rowlands adopted
Stanley's name. He fought on both sides in the American Civil

War, then became a travelling journalist, revisiting St Asaph's workhouse posing as a Civil War hero in an officer's uniform he had bought during a disastrous trip to Turkey.

Stanley wrote sensational accounts of the Native American wars, the Suez Canal construction and the British attack on Abyssinia, in the latter case bribing the telegraph operator to send his copy first to scoop his competitors. The proprietor of the *Herald*, James Gordon Bennett Jr, commissioned him to find Livingstone in December 1868, after he had been in Africa for two-and-a-half years without word. It was thought that having discovered the source of the Nile, Livingstone would follow it to Egypt, so the assignment at this point was simply to wait for his imminent arrival there and debrief him. Stanley spent two months in Egypt without finding a scrap of information about Livingstone's journey, and gave up. In fact at this point Livingstone was travelling with Bogharib and bin Saleh from Lake Bangweulu to Tanganyika and at death's door.

Bennett met Stanley in Paris in October 1869 and sent him to find Livingstone wherever he was. According to Stanley's doubtless romanticized account in *How I Found Livingstone*, when he warned his employer of the cost, Bennett replied, "Well, I will tell you what you will do. Draw a thousand pounds now; and when you have gone through that, draw another thousand, and when that is spent, draw another thousand, and when you have finished that, draw another thousand, and so on; but, FIND LIVINGSTONE."

Bennett gave Stanley other reports to write on the way, so he travelled via the Crimea, Palestine and Persia, arriving in Zanzibar in January 1871, while Livingstone was in Mamohela waiting for the Banian slaves to arrive. Stanley kept the purpose of his journey completely secret, but assembled a large, well-equipped expedition. In wild contrast to Livingstone, he travelled with 160 porters and twenty-seven donkeys carrying six tons of equipment and supplies, twenty-three soldiers and fifty guns, and two British sailors.

Hearing a rumour that Livingstone was near Tanganyika, Stanley went directly west, covering the 400 miles to the Arab station at Unyanyembe in three months. The expedition suffered the familiar trials of mud and malaria, theft and dysentery. Stanley used a dog whip on "the lazily-inclined". At Unyanyembe he found letters for Livingstone, along with the crew Kirk had sent to deliver supplies, and seeing they had little interest in reaching their destination, took command of them. The route westwards was blocked by local armies defending their land against the slavers of Unyanyembe. Stanley joined forces with the slavers in an attempt to get through the blockade, but they were routed and Stanley ended up defending Unyanyembe in a siege.

He continued with a crew reduced to fifty-four, leaving behind Kirk's delivery for Livingstone, and circumvented the Nyamwezi blockade. Hearing on the road that Livingstone had returned to Ujiji, Stanley approached the town with a fifty-gun salute and the US flag carried high. This brought a thousand people out to meet them, including bin Saleh, Bogharib, Susi and Chuma, and Stanley had to push his way through the crowd to get to Livingstone's house.

> *What would I not have given for a bit of friendly wilderness, where, unseen, I might vent my joy in some mad freak, such as idiotically biting my hand, turning a somersault, or slashing at trees, in order to allay those exciting feelings that were well-nigh uncontrollable. My heart beats fast, but I must not let my face betray my emotions, lest it shall detract from the dignity of a white man appearing under such extraordinary circumstances.* [26]

Thus Stanley – who in publishing this account became infamous with British literati for his vulgar sensationalism – uttered the classic expression of Victorian reserve. The paradox is increased by the fact that he printed it in capitals. He continues:

> *I would have run to him, only I was a coward in the*
> *presence of such a mob – would have embraced him,*
> *but that I did not know how he would receive me; so*
> *I did what moral cowardice and false pride suggested*
> *was the best thing – walked deliberately to him, took*
> *off my hat, and said:*
> *"DR. LIVINGSTONE, I PRESUME?"* [27]

Like most great quotations, it is debated whether he ever said it, but there is no good reason to deny it, though one might suspect that the line was more premeditated than he suggests. It became the most quoted phrase of the era, the constant refrain of music hall acts and magazines, and Stanley came to hate being introduced to new acquaintances and hearing the inevitable, "Mr Stanley, I presume?" By then, though, it had made his fortune.

Livingstone of course was overjoyed, in his equally reserved way, to see Stanley, with his supplies, equipment, letters and means of transport. He was overwhelmed with gratitude to Bennett. They shared a bottle of champagne, and Stanley told him the news of the world – the Franco-Prussian War and the fall of Napoleon III, the transatlantic telegraph, the Suez Canal. Livingstone read that the British government had voted his expedition £1,000. The pair got on extraordinarily well, laughing, talking at length and eating four meals a day. Livingstone told his multitude of African stories and Stanley lapped them up. He expounded on "the Nile problem" and the peoples of Africa. He recounted the Nyangwe massacre with "real passion in his language and an angry glitter in his eyes", though he also dwelt with embarrassing intensity on the benighted individuals he had fallen out with throughout his life. Stanley quickly learned that when Livingstone became absorbed in his thoughts, staring into the distance and moving his lips silently, it was a bad idea to intrude.

They spent a happy fortnight in Ujiji, and Livingstone quickly felt a great deal better, so he wanted to get back to work. He asked Stanley to take him back to the Lualaba, but Stanley said his men would never go that far, suggesting that instead they should sail to the north end of Tanganyika and settle the question as to whether a river flows north out of it.

They went in a large rowing boat, and faced hostile tribes when they stopped at night. Stanley, whose journey to Ujiji had been delayed by ruinous demands for tolls, was impressed to see how Livingstone met such demands with calm, good-humoured requests for food. They were once robbed as they slept and more than once attacked by would-be robbers throwing stones. Stanley's instinct was to shoot, but he was stopped by an implicit sense that Livingstone would disapprove. They reached the river on 27 November 1871, in what is now Burundi. Livingstone was disappointed to see that it flowed into, not out of, the lake, and concluded rightly that the lake must drain westwards into the Lualaba. It was a body blow for his cherished Nile theory; but as he still hoped against hope that the Lualaba was the Nile, it was not dead yet.

They went together east to Unyanyembe, because Stanley was keen to see the great traveller in action, and he offered Livingstone the use of his house and stores there while he waited for Stanley to go to Zanzibar and send a team of reliable porters from there. Livingstone could also collect Kirk's deliveries which Stanley had left there. Stanley was not disappointed in Livingstone's journeying. The "man of iron" suffered painful bleeding feet, but refused to ride a donkey. In January, they were attacked by a swarm of bees. Livingstone, unable to run as fast as the others, threw himself into a bush to escape. He was "stung dreadfully in the head and in the face," Stanley reported; "the bees had settled in handfuls in his hair." As they had already walked eighteen miles that day, Stanley tried to persuade him to be carried in a stretcher, but Livingstone insisted on walking to the camp, where "after partaking of a cup of warm tea and some food, he was as cheerful as if he had never travelled a mile." On another occasion, Livingstone intervened to stop Stanley beating his cook in an argument over unwashed coffee pots.

Reaching Unyanyembe in February 1872, they found the stores had been reduced by thieves and white ants, but Stanley gave most of his things to Livingstone, who found himself better equipped than he had been for years. Stanley urged Livingstone to come home to Britain with him, and convalesce properly before returning to his work, but Livingstone would not hear of it, quoting with pride a letter from his dear Agnes: "Much as I wish you to come home, I would rather that you finished your work to your own satisfaction than return merely to gratify me."

They stayed a month there, Livingstone writing letters and a legible version of his journal. He talked as ardently as ever of finding the Nile sources, but told one friend, "If indeed my disclosures should lead to the suppression of the East Coast slave-trade, I should esteem that as a far greater feat than the discovery of all the sources together." He wrote two rather tart letters to Kirk, doubtless feeling that Stanley's triumphant rescue put Kirk's unsuccessful efforts in a rather poor light. He contrasted Kirk's employment of useless slaves with Stanley's efficient management of free labour, instructed Kirk to hand over the official funds for Livingstone's relief to Stanley to spend on his behalf, give Stanley every assistance, and to cancel or recall any expedition he may have planned himself. "I may wait twenty years and your slaves feast and fail."

Stanley stopped asking Livingstone for stories of the Zambezi expedition, because of the disenchanting rancour they brought with them. "I felt the faintest fear that his strong nature was opposed to forgiveness and that he was not so perfect as at the first blush of friendship I thought him." Still, though, he wrote adoringly of Livingstone's gentleness, manliness and nobility, saying that "each day witnessed a sermon acted". Livingstone talked to Stanley of his continued hope for African mission despite the false starts he had seen, and said he believed there was one overarching purpose to his life which explained why he had been "led away, here and there, and crossed and baffled over and over again, to wear out my years and strength. Why was it, but to be a witness of the full horror of this slave-trade?... My business is to publish what I see, to rouse up those who have power to stop it, once and for all."

When Stanley was ready to go, it was Livingstone's turn to try to make him stay, and Stanley's to insist that the sooner he reached Zanzibar, the sooner Livingstone would get his porters and continue with his work. On the eve of parting, Livingstone finally gave voice to his gratitude in such an outpouring that Stanley broke down and sobbed. The next morning, 14 March, they shared breakfast but neither could eat. Stanley overcame an urge to hug Livingstone at the last moment, but failed to turn away before the tears started again. "I betrayed myself!" he says. All Livingstone's journal has to say is: "Mr Stanley leaves. I commit to his care my journal sealed with five seals... Positively not to be opened."

Chapter 26

LAST STEPS

Having months to wait at Unyanyembe for the men Stanley was to send, Livingstone filled his time preparing for the journey. He planned to go to the southern side of the southernmost lake of the watershed and follow the watercourse north. He bought cows, made cheese, ground flour, tarred his tent, made a plumb line. In his journal he noted the progress of a nearby war, and how local boys made toy guns from reeds. He heard that 200 of Dugumbe's men had been killed in the expedition he nearly joined them on, again confirming that God's good hand had been in the thwarting of his plans. Scenes of atrocities he had witnessed still made him "start up at dead of night, horrified by their vividness".

He made detailed plans for a Christian mission station near the coast, suggesting that Anglo-Catholics, "who at home amuse themselves with fastings", should take up the call to this hungry land, and put their self-indulgent self-denials to some use. He urged those who read his journal to consider the vocation, and not to believe all the bad things they heard about Africans: "Devoting yourselves heartily to the savages, as they are called, you will find, with some drawbacks and wickednesses, a very great deal to admire and love." He denied that they would be won round by displays of the "jugglery" of European technology: "they have too much good sense for that. … Goodness or unselfishness impresses their minds more."

He wrote to *The New York Herald*, outlining the horrors of the east African so-called slave trade – "they are not traded for, but murdered for" – though all he could say of the scenes he had witnessed in Nyangwe is that they "were so sickening I cannot allow the mind to dwell upon them or write about them". He explained that the process was entirely dependent on the Zanzibar market and demanded that the great powers close it: "All I can say in my solitude is, may Heaven's rich blessing come down on every one American, English, Turk who will help to heal this Open Sore of the World."

As for finding the source of the Nile, his writing swung between a sense that he had been steered by God through countless dangers for the sake of this last great quasi-biblical mission, and creeping doubts. "I am oppressed with the apprehension that after all it may turn out that I have been following the Congo; and who would risk being put into a cannibal pot, and converted into black man for it?" This disappointing resort to the *Punch* cartoon image of Africans is particularly worth quoting, both to show that Livingstone was capable of it, alongside his more enlightened comments, and also as a reminder of how consistently far he generally steered from such a stereotype of the British in Africa.

In June 1872, Livingstone heard that another expedition had been sent to find him, this one organized by the Royal Geographical Society, on Kirk's urging. It was led by two naval officers, and the third-in-command was Livingstone's nineteen-year-old son, Oswell. They had reached the African mainland from Zanzibar just as Stanley's first report came through. Concluding that a second rescue would be superfluous, the expedition was disbanded, but Oswell sent his father a letter before returning. It said – so David told Agnes – that Oswell's purpose in coming had been to bring him back to his "forgotten family" and get money off him to complete his medical training, and that Oswell was returning without him because the government had granted David more funds, which Oswell thought he could access in England. His attitude seemed to David to compare dismally with that of Stanley – his actual son with his spiritual son, one might say. He told Agnes he was "as poor a specimen of a son as Africa ever produced".

David was also distressed to hear from Oswell that he was widely reported to have made a damning attack on Kirk's character. This was in fact the work of Stanley, who stated publicly, in the talks he gave around Britain about his African adventure, that "he had a mission from Livingstone to describe Kirk as a traitor", and that Livingstone believed he should be dismissed. It was true that Livingstone was disappointed in Kirk's efforts to send assistance, as his letter to Kirk plainly said, but Stanley went way beyond the truth. He had taken a violent dislike to Kirk at Zanzibar, from what seems like a jealousy of Livingstone's former favourite young travelling companion. His lie was believed by everyone – reasonably enough considering Livingstone's emotional track record – including those who knew Kirk did not deserve the attack. Oswell wrote to *The Telegraph* to defend Kirk from his father, and Waller wrote in protest to Livingstone – a letter he never received. Livingstone meanwhile assumed the fuss had arisen from Kirk's overreaction to his letter, and wrote a conciliatory response to both Kirk and the Foreign Office, saying in the latter, "I regret very much to hear incidentally that Dr. Kirk viewed my formal complaint against Banians as a covert attack upon himself. If I had foreseen this, I should certainly have borne my losses in silence. I never had any difference with him." However, it took an official inquiry by Frere to clear Kirk's name.

Fifty-seven of Stanley's men finally reached Livingstone in August. They joined Livingstone's other helpers: Chuma and Amoda, their two wives, Susi and Gardner, and Mabruki, another of the Nasik students who had rejoined him. David wrote to Agnes that he was leaving in the hope of achieving the immeasurable good of ending the slave trade. "This will be something to have lived for, and the conviction has grown in my mind that it was for this end I have been detained so long."

They left on 25 August 1872, and Livingstone quickly found that all his rest and good food had not restored him to health. He suffered chronic dysentery and lost a lot of blood. The heat was increasingly oppressive and by November, as they approached the base of Tanganyika, the scorched ground burnt their feet. Crossing the River Kalambo, Livingstone missed discovering one of the highest waterfalls in Africa, the Kalambo Falls, by a matter of miles. The oppressive heat then gave way to oppressive rain and cold, but Livingstone decided his crew were as good as Makololo, adding, "I cannot award them higher praise."

During one rainy delay, David wrote a rare letter to his brother John in Ontario, whom he had not seen since he first came to Africa. "If the good Lord permits me to put a stop to the enormous evils of the inland slave-trade, I shall not grudge my hunger and toils. I shall bless His name with all my heart. The Nile sources are valuable to me only as a means of enabling me to open my mouth with power among men."

The rain and cold grew worse still in January 1873, but they crossed the Urungu hills near Lake Bangweulu pretty much on schedule. From here, though, the going became tortuous. The ground was waterlogged and leech-ridden, the "most fatiguing, plunging, deep sponge". The weather made navigational observations impossible and they had to rely on Livingstone's original mistaken longitudes. Villagers were too suspicious to give them reliable guidance. In words that sound plaintive and fragile coming from the celebrated explorer, he wrote on 23 January: "I don't know where we are." The following day they crossed a 300-yard river, and Livingstone had to be carried piggy back in shifts. Susi took the first turn, the water coming up to his mouth. Livingstone had a growing sense that he would not survive the journey.

Finally reaching the east side of the flooded lake on 13 February, he sent Susi and Chuma to Matipa's town to hire canoes to take them south, but the travellers were not where they thought they were and it took the pair of them two weeks to find the town. While Livingstone waited, he was attacked by red ants, suffered bleeding piles, and killed their last goat. But the first leg of the journey was completed, and Livingstone's sense of doom faded. He wrote to James Young, "I seem to see the end to which I have been striving looming in the distance." He asked Waller to book lodgings near Regent's Park for him and Agnes and make a dentist's appointment. He said he hoped to see Waller a bishop and would give him the kiss of peace "with a smack that will make the rafters ring, and girls all giggle, and Mrs. Waller jealous".

Susi and Chuma agreed a price with Chief Matipa, but no canoes came, so Livingstone went to the island himself on 27 February. He was still waiting there on 19 March, his sixtieth birthday. He wrote in his journal: "Thanks to the Almighty Preserver of men for sparing me thus far on the journey of life. Can I hope for ultimate success? So many obstacles have arisen. Let not Satan prevail over me, Oh! my good Lord Jesus!" That day, as they had only received one of the canoes, Livingstone resorted to a show of force. He went into Matipa's house, fired a gun through the roof and called his men. Matipa fled, Livingstone sent presents after him, and three more canoes duly came. Most of the party still had to wade along the lakeside.

It was hard going, in "pitiless pelting rain", and by April Livingstone was bleeding profusely. "I am pale, bloodless, and weak…" he wrote on 10 May. "Oh, how I long to be permitted by the Over Power to finish my work." Soon the rain stopped, the wind dropped, the sky cleared and the villages became more friendly, but Livingstone was increasingly too weak to walk or even ride a donkey and had to be carried. On 27 May, after four days when the only entry was the date, he made his last journal entry: "Knocked up quite and remain – recover – sent to buy milch goats. We are on the banks of the R. Molilamo."

Two days later they came to Chitambo's, twenty miles from the southernmost point of Lake Bangweulu, Susi running ahead to arrange the building of a hut for Livingstone. When Chitambo visited him the next day, Livingstone could not speak. An hour before midnight Livingstone was woken by shouting and asked Susi if his men were creating a disturbance. Susi said the villagers were driving a buffalo away from their crops. Livingstone asked where they were, then, *"Sikun'gapi kuenda Luapula?"* ("How many days to the Luapula?") Susi replied, *"Na zani zikutatu, Bwana."* ("I think three days, master.") Livingstone sighed in pain, "Oh dear, dear!" and then went back to sleep. At midnight he asked for boiled water and calomel.

At four in the morning, 1 May 1873, Majwara, the boy watching him, called Susi and Chuma. They found Livingstone kneeling by the side of his bed, his hands on the pillow. They assumed he was praying, but the Majwara said he had slept for a long time and woken to find him in the same position as when he went to sleep. One of them touched his cheek, and then they lifted him onto the bed and covered him. Whatever his last words were, they were not heard by or addressed to human ears.

Chapter 27

THE LONG RUN

It seems impertinent to pry into the utmost privacy of David Livingstone's last prayer, even in imagination. But having accompanied him – or followed his tracks – this far, we can at least form an idea of the state of mind in which he faced the end of his life.

"We are immortal till our work is done," he had said, and yet it would not take an unreasonable degree of pessimism to say that the three great concerns that dominated Livingstone's life – evangelism, exploration and abolition – all ended in failure. He had failed to discover the source of the Nile after spending seven years going after it like the grail, and if he had been given the extra years he yearned for, it would only have been to discover that it was not there. But at least where exploration was concerned he could look back on a long list of earlier triumphs: Ngami, Dilolo, Victoria Falls, Shirwa and Nyasa, the Batoka plateau and Shire highlands, and mapping an entire cross section of Africa. Even during the frustrations of his last expedition he had added Mweru and Bangweulu to the list. When it comes to evangelism, though, estimates of the number of people he converted in his entire career vary between one and none, and the end result of his opening Africa to other missionaries was the "chaplaincy to a consulate" on Zanzibar. Worst of all, his efforts to fight the slave trade had simply helped it to double in size. The way the horror of the trade so dominated his thoughts, words and deeds during this last expedition – when his only obligation to his sponsors was exploration – does at least finally answer the question of his true motivation: this was every bit as important to him as exploration. But that just makes it a more important failure.

And yet it seems safe to say this was not the tone of Livingstone's last reflections. "We are immortal" was not for him a guarantee that all his plans would be fulfilled, but a belief that all God's (better informed) plans would be fulfilled. It meant that whatever God required of him, he would be allowed to do, and whatever he was not allowed to do was not required of him. It meant that failure was not an option. Success was God's and what belonged to Livingstone was to obey his call and play his part. Livingstone did that. The question of ultimate success was simply none of his business.

This must have been a reassuring thought to Livingstone – as it is to those who look back on his life sympathetically today – because without it the way in which his failures were turned into such success so swiftly after he was out of earshot would seem rather heartless.

Livingstone's crew buried his heart and other organs in a flour tin on the banks of Bangweulu, and the best at English among the crew, Jacob Wainwright of Nasik, read the Prayer Book service for the burial of the dead. They preserved his body in salt and carried it towards Zanzibar along with his papers. The journey was, of course, no less an ordeal without Livingstone than it would have been with him – swamp, disease and attacks from men and lions. At Unyanyembe, they met the latest Livingstone search party, whose leading officer wanted to bury the body there. They successfully resisted, though he commandeered Livingstone's instruments. At the coast they were met by Lieutenant Prideaux, Kirk's deputy. He paid the men their wages, gave the women nothing, and dismissed them all, apart from Wainwright, whom, on the basis of his English, Prideaux sent to England with the body.

Livingstone was buried in Westminster Abbey on 18 April 1874. The coffin, bearing a wreath from the Queen, was carried by Wainwright, Stanley, Waller, Young, Kirk, Webb, Oswell and Steele. Robert Moffat, seventy-nine years old, walked behind the coffin with Thomas and Oswell Livingstone. Agnes was seated with David's sisters Janet and Agnes, who were in England for the first time. The government paid for the funeral and gave £3,000 to Livingstone's family.

That year, Waller brought Chuma and Susi to England to help him produce the *Last Journals of David Livingstone* and supplement his records with their own stories. The public for the first time read Livingstone's account of the Nyangwe massacre and its connection to the east coast slave trade, but by that time the trade was finished, through a process in which Livingstone and his allies were the key players.

In 1869, Lord Clarendon, on the strength of Livingstone's reports, had led a House of Lords inquiry into the Zanzibar slave trade, which recommended pressing the Sultan, the ruler of Zanzibar, to gradually diminish it. In 1870, Waller joined the Anti-Slavery Committee, which organized pressure on the government for more decisive action. A Commons inquiry followed in 1871, hearing from Frere and Waller, but above all leaning on Livingstone's accounts. It reported on 4 August, concluding that all east coast slave trading went through Zanzibar, and demanding the Sultan be told he had to end it immediately or British ships would end it for him. The Foreign Secretary got international backing. Public pressure backed official action: in July 1872 the Anti-Slavery Society held a large rally, and *The Times* called for an abolition treaty with Zanzibar, both brandishing Livingstone's name. Only then did Livingstone's despatches and newspaper letters mentioning the Nyangwe massacre arrive; they did not go into details but Stanley supplemented them. On 27 September, the Foreign Secretary appointed Frere to negotiate abolition with the Sultan. Before he left, Frere addressed a huge anti-slavery rally alongside Waller, Stanley, Moffat, and Thomas Fowell Buxton, grandson of the man who had first set Livingstone on this road. Waller spent the winter touring the country drumming up petitions, while Frere joined Kirk in Zanzibar. When the Sultan refused to stop the trade, Frere, overstepping his remit, threatened a blockade, and Kirk got the Sultan's signature on 5 June 1873, five weeks after Livingstone's death. The Zanzibar slave market closed and the east coast trade, which enslaved 18,000 people a year and killed far more, was finished.

Six years later, the African Lakes Corporation completed Livingstone's abolition design by putting a steamer called the *Lady Nyassa* on Lake Nyasa, to engage in legitimate trade with local people. By the end of the century the company had seventeen steamers, plus smaller boats, on Nyasa, the Zambesi, the Shire, Tanganyika and Mweru.

It has often been said that Livingstone's revelation of the Nyangwe massacre is what closed the Zanzibar slave market. As good a story as that would be, the chronology above shows that it is not quite right. The most that could be claimed for the Nyangwe story is that it gave additional firepower to the last charge in a battle that was already all but won. But that makes no difference to the greatness of Livingstone's achievement, because it was his reports on the slave trade from earlier in his last journey, and before, that had won that battle.

As for evangelism, within two years of Livingstone's death, a new mission inspired by him was en route to Nyasa, under the name of Livingstonia. It was led by, of all people, James Stewart, last seen throwing his copy of *Missionary Travels* into the Zambezi, who underwent a reconversion to Livingstonism at the funeral. The first Christian conversion at Livingstonia took six years; they did not learn about perseverance from Livingstone. By the first year of the twentieth century, that mission had five churches with a total of 1,576 members, and that year they baptized 563 people. Their doctors treated 19,000 patients a year. True to Livingstone's ideals, they had 531 black preachers and a training institute. The army of native agents that he dreamed of throughout his life was finally realized by his death.

Livingstonia did not stand alone. It was quickly followed by a mission on the Shire highlands called Blantyre. The Universities Mission returned from Zanzibar to the mainland in 1875. The CMS established its east African mission in what is now Uganda as a result of Stanley's expedition to complete Livingstone's exploration of the Lualaba.

These developments could only be considered an unambiguous monument if the British presence in Africa over the following century had been thoroughly benign, rather than a muddle of paternalism, invasion, development, subjugation and exploitation. Within twenty years of Livingstone's death, as a result of the mission and trading stations there, Nyasaland and Uganda were ruled by the British crown, the Sultan's territories were divided between Britain and Germany despite Frere's treaty, Stanley had helped King Leopold II establish his slave colony in the Congo, which halved the population of 20 million in forty years, and in 1893 Cecil Rhodes' machine guns mowed down 1,500 Matabele for their goldfields – four times the casualties of the Nyangwe massacre. In Livingstone's defence, the reality of European imperialism was nothing like the local community presence that he – so critical of British policy in the Cape – had envisaged when he talked of a colony. And yet the summons to Africa that he issued was clearly, however unintentionally, one of the causes of that scramble.

All these were very public and widely recognized repercussions of Livingstone's career. Unnoticed at the time, however, and generally unnoticed since, one more important story had been unfolding alongside them.

When the Matabele mission instigated by Livingstone arrived at its destination in 1859, astonishingly they found that the tribe already had regular Christian prayers. The missionary who had beaten the British to it was Sechele. After the Livingstones left him, Sechele had decided to lead the Bakwena's services and teach at their school, preaching, praying, reading the Bible and leading them in "some old psalm tune greatly mutilated", as Moffat sniffed. Sechele encouraged others who could read, including his wife and daughters, to help. Bible reading became popular. Sechele travelled hundreds of miles as a missionary and had considerable success, but was still so keen to have a European missionary with the Bakwena that he asked the Boer commandant for one and was sent three Germans. After a demarcation dispute, they were replaced by LMS missionaries: Roger Price of the disastrous Makololo mission and his second wife, Elizabeth, Mary Livingstone's sister.

Sechele became the most powerful Tswana king, as, having withstood the Boers, the Bakwena became a refuge for other tribes. By 1860, they had absorbed nine other tribes, and on his death in 1892 he ruled 30,000 people, a hundred times the number with which Livingstone had first found him. When Sekomi of the Bamangwato died, Sechele intervened to ensure his Christian son Khama succeeded him. In the estimation of Neil Parsons of the University of Botswana, Sechele "did more to propagate Christianity in nineteenth-century southern Africa than virtually any single European missionary".

The various missionaries who knew Sechele agreed that he was a frustrating puzzle, "a half Christian and a half heathen" in the words of Thomas Morgan Thomas of the Matabele mission. He returned to rainmaking, considering it a political necessity, and late in life returned to polygamy, marrying a young woman for what do not seem to have been entirely political reasons. He used traditional "charms and incantations, washings and purifyings", and missionaries were appalled to see a list of his ancestors on the church wall. And yet, as Elizabeth Price – who heartily hated him – admitted, "he reads the Bible threadbare", and when confronted he ran scriptural rings around them. "Roger had to keep his wits about him," she wrote, "or he would have been [lo]st, so wily and cunning is Sechele – murdering sacred scripture and bringing it to defend him in a way which horrifies and amazes one. A strange, strange mixture he is!"

The strange mixture was in fact African Christianity. Unlike other converts who were content to follow European Christianity, Sechele went back to the source and recreated it as an indigenous religion. Modern commentators have also been puzzled, wondering what motivated his conversion. As politically advantageous as it proved eventually, it would have taken miraculous powers to foresee that, when he was contemplating the renunciation of rainmaking and polygamy. The simplest explanation is the most obvious: he converted to Christianity because David Livingstone convinced him that it was true.

It would be stretching a point to give Livingstone full credit for Sechele's extraordinary missionary career, but it is at least a fitting end to the story that began with him coming to Africa wanting above all to make African missionaries. And it is one last piece in the puzzle of Livingstone's life, which even if complete could hardly be said to be solved. He was the great explorer whose greatest mission turned out to be a mirage; the abolitionist who rooted out the slave trade only to make way for imperialism; and the missionary whose contribution to the conversion of Africa was at once too small and too large to measure. As a man he was heroic and petty, humane and harsh, unconquerably dauntless while on the move but a serial defeatist if supposed to stay put, and a loving husband and father who gave his family back to Jesus. Nothing about who he was is straightforward; it is not surprising that the same is true for what he left behind.

ENDNOTES

1. SOAS, CWM/LMS Archives, Africa Odds, Box 2, January 1838.
2. As previous.
3. David Livingstone, *Missionary Travels and Researches in South Africa* (London: John Murray, 1857), p. 8.
4. William G. Blaikie, *The Personal Life of David Livingstone* (London: John Murray, 1880), pp. 34-35.
5. As previous, p. 36.
6. Isaac Schapera (ed.), *Livingstone's Missionary Correspondence 1841–1856* (London: Chatto & Windus, 1961), p. 18.
7. As previous, pp. 122–23.
8. As previous, p. 190.
9. Mitchell Library, James Cowie Collection, MS.301, http://www.livingstoneonline.ucl.ac.uk/view/transcript.php?id=LETT302.
10. Livingstone, *Missionary Travels and Researches*, pp. 118–19.
11. The Commandant mentions only three killed and six wounded. He also claimed the attack was provoked by "repeated threats and intimidating conduct".
12. George Seaver, *David Livingstone: His Life and Letters* (New York: Harper, 1957), p. 233.
13. As previous, p. 256.
14. *The United Presbyterian Magazine*, volume 1, number 12 (December 1857), p. 550.
15. Adam Sedgwick and William Monk (ed.) *Dr. Livingstone's Cambridge Lectures* (Cambridge: 1860), p. 168.
16. In an 1862 letter, Kirk mentions Rae giving Baines a certificate acquitting him of the shirt theft he had accused him of, but it is not clear whether that happened now or later.
17. *The Missionary Magazine and Chronicle*, volume 25, number 18 (1861), p. 165.
18. Seaver, *David Livingstone: His Life and Letters*, p. 412.
19. Reginald Foskett (ed.), *The Zambesi Journal and Letters of Dr. John Kirk 1858–63* (Edinburgh: Oliver and Boyd, 1965), vol. II, p. 475.
20. David Livingstone, *Narrative of an expedition to the Zambesi and its tributaries* (London: John Murray: 1865), pp. 449–50.
21. Tim Jeal, *David Livingstone* (London: Heinemann, 1973), p. 280.
22. Blaikie, *The Personal Life of David Livingstone*, pp. 349–50.
23. *The Fortnightly Review*, volume 4 (1866), p. 103.
24. Horace Waller, *The Last Journals of David Livingstone* (London: John Murray, 1874), vol. I, pp. 169, 172.
25. As previous, vol. I, 306.
26. Henry M. Stanley *How I Found Livingstone* (London: Sampson, Low, Marston, Searle & Rivington, 1890), p. 830.

INDEX